By Christopher Dow

Fiction
Effigy
    Book I: Stroud
    Book II: Oakdale
The Books of Bob
    Devil of a Time
    Jumping Jehovah
The Clay Guthrie Mysteries
    The Dead Detective
    Landscape with Beast
    The Texas Troll Unlimited
    Darkness Insatiable
Roadkill
The Werewolf and Tide, and Other Compulsions

Nonfiction
Lord of the Loincloth (nonfiction novel)
Book of Curiosities: Adventures in the Paranormal
Occasional Pilgrimage: Essays on Film, Literature, and Other Matters
Living the Story: The Meandering, True, and Sometimes Strange
        Adventures of an Unknown Writer, Vols. I & II

Poetry
City of Dreams
The Trip Out
Texas White Line Fever
Networks
A Dilapidation of Machinery
Puzzle Pieces: Selected Poems

Art
Harboring with Arabesques: The Art of Christopher Dow

Martial Arts
The Wellspring: An Inquiry into the Nature of Chi
Circling the Square: Observations on the Dynamics of Tai Chi Chuan
Elements of Power: Essays on the Art and Practice of Tai Chi Chuan
Alchemy of Breath: An Introduction to Chi Kung
Leaves on the Wind: A Survey of Martial Arts Literature, Vols. I–VI

Editor
Drifts: Texas Writers: Interviews and Profiles
The Abby Stone: The Poetry of Bartholo Dias
The Best of Phosphene
The Best of Dialog

THE BEST OF
DIALOG

THE BEST OF
DIALOG

COMPILED AND EDITED BY
CHRISTOPHER DOW

Phosphene Publishing Company
Temple, Texas

CONTENTS

Foreword —— 13

POETRY

James Bettison
    After . . . Dinner . . . Thought . . . —— 19
R. T. Castleberry
    Sketch for Mourning —— 20
Robert Dante
    Lessons in Charm —— 21
    The Persistence of Memory —— 22
Claire Donohue-Korolenko
    Pecan Day —— 23
Christopher Dow
    Fall Flies —— 24
Lisa Howell Fenton
    After Reading Ayn Rand —— 26
Lisa Goodman
    Sitting on a Couch with an Absent Jazzman —— 28
Nina Haas
    Impatience —— 30
Kristin Higgins
    The Sculptor Manque —— 31
Lyn Lifshin
    My Sister's Diaries —— 32
Virginia Long
    Remembered Fragrance —— 33
Phillip Lopate
    Straight Man —— 34
John Lunstroth
    untitled —— 37
Orson T. Maquelani
    On a Lover's Bridge to Reality —— 39

Elizabeth McBride
    The Atoll —— 40
    Kwajalein —— 41
    Shells —— 42
Robin McCorquodale
    Andres Segovia, We Want to Show You Our
        Henry Moore —— 43
    The Promise —— 45
Joan McNearney
    an executive —— 48
D. Meeks
    Bing Cherries, Purple Plums —— 49
    Seachange —— 51
Vassar Miller
    Fear —— 52
    A Rage for Order for Rose —— 53
    Sleep —— 54
    What *Really* Happens —— 55
Harryette Mullen
    A Brand of Love —— 56
Marie Ponsot
    Metro Bus —— 57
    Museum —— 59
Pattiann Rogers
    The Myth of the Fields —— 61
    A Sequence of Circumstances —— 63
    Remembering the Imagination: A Love Letter —— 65
Jacqueline Simon
    The Biloxi Shrimper Confesses to His
        Monsignor —— 67
    The Monsignor Replies to the Shrimper —— 68

Sidney Wade
    French Lilacs —— 69
    Two Leaves —— 70
Christopher Woods
    Tennessee —— 71

FICTION

Marie Dybala
    A Rose for Anna —— 75
Billie Sue Mosiman
    Wild Strawberries —— 83
Marsha Carter
    Nothing but the Blood —— 93
Lionel Garcia
    The Wedding —— 101
Frances Fletcher
    The Perfect Gift —— 113
Enid Jimenez
    Locked In/Looked Out —— 125
Christopher Dow
    Meeting with Arthur —— 137
Tracey Nichols
    The Storm —— 153
Jim Hendrick
    Bird the Good —— 167
Richard M. Bolling
    Easter Tuesday —— 181

Essay

Phillip Lopate
    In the Here and Now —— 195

THE BEST OF
DIALOG

Foreword

You'd think that folks who had already published one failed literary magazine would have learned to leave well enough alone. But *Phosphene* had not failed in a critical sense, only a financial one, and that because we were trying to survive solely off of the sale of copies. The *Phosphene* story is related in the foreword to *The Best of Phosphene*, however, and we're not here to talk about it, per se, but about what happened beginning a year or so after its demise.

It was about then that Steven Robinson, Lazaro Aleman, and I were again bitten by the publishing bug. Or maybe I should say that we relapsed. Publishing is, I think, rather like malaria—you get bitten once and suffer recurring bouts of varying intensity for the remainder of your life. In fact, Lazaro and I both went on to become professional editors and writers. Sometimes, I've learned, you actually manage to publish something worthwhile, but most of the time, it all just seems like a fever dream.

As the three of us began discussions, we generally agreed that our new endeavor had to be structured differently from *Phosphene*. First, the new magazine had to pay for itself. We had paid to produce *Phosphene*, but that magazine died because we were doomed to continue paying. We wanted the new magazine eventually to make its own way financially, though we understood that, initially, we'd have to pay to produce it. With that in mind, we took in a fourth partner, Richard Leach. Rick did not have a background in writing or art, but he was intrigued by the endeavor, and he assumed the role of general business manager.

The format of *Phosphene* had not allowed for any sort of income aside from direct sales or subscriptions. Making the new magazine pay for itself entailed a different approach in both form and format, and we decided to produce it as a newsprint tabloid. This had the principal advantage of cheaper production costs with a greater press run—we could print 10,000 copies of a tabloid for about the same amount as producing 1,000 copies of *Phosphene*. In addition, with that format, we could sell advertising space to finance the endeavor. To ensure readership, we would give the tabloid away for free at various outlets in Houston's Inner Loop.

The idea wasn't farfetched. This was during the early 1980s, and the first boom in free inner-city tabloids was under way—one free Houston tabloid, *Innerview*, already was out there and holding its own. We didn't feel that there would be any problems between us and the publisher of *Innerview* since that tabloid carried news and viewpoints, and we were targeting a different, though overlapping, readership.

There remained only one more task before we began to publish—naming the new magazine. We knew right from the start that we would not be using *Phosphene*. That publication had played its hand, and we wanted a fresh name to go with our fresh approach. We mulled it over for a couple of weeks, when one afternoon, within an hour of each other, both Lazaro and I independently came up with the name *Dialog*. It seemed to symbolize what we were after—interaction within the literary community, with the community at large, and between writer and reader. The symbolism and the synchronicity were too much to ignore, and the new publication was christened.

Dialog began as an extension of *Phosphene*, and to provide content for the first couple of issues, we put back into harness the stable of writers and artists we had developed with the earlier magazine. Soon, however, we expanded beyond our original staples of poetry, fiction, essays, art, and photography to include articles, book reviews, and interviews with notable writers, Texas and otherwise. Ten thousand copies brings a lot of visibility, and that, in turn, brought greater attention. Ad sales were only modest, but they provided enough supplemental income to allow us to run poetry and fiction contests with cash prizes. The fiction contest brought in some particularly good work.

Alas, ad sales never completely managed to pay for *Dialog*'s production. None of us were good at sales, and the ads we did get came rather haphazardly. Making *Dialog* pay for itself would have entailed a single-minded attention to ad sales that none of us possessed, and so, financially, *Dialog* floundered into its second year and never saw its third.

But it never floundered in an artistic sense, though we did manage to publish some material that didn't make it into this volume. In the year and a half that *Dialog* was alive, we pushed the boundaries that we'd set with *Phosphene* into wider spheres of readership and literary community. The 10,000 copies always disappeared fast, and we received a lot of nice mail along with submissions.

But *Dialog* did expire. Not only were ad sales mediocre, but the lives and personal focuses of the editors changed, too. After a year and a half, we rather suddenly called it quits. While I admit that, at the time, I was ready for a break, I was sorry to see *Dialog* go. Given adequate support by better ad sales, it could have survived and matured to give the Houston literary scene a more constant and long-lived voice. Since *Dialog*'s demise, several other Houston publications have offered a bit of the literary—such as *Blonde on Blonde*—but none have lasted long. I used to believe that it still could happen—that someday someone who is better organized and better funded will accomplish where we failed. But the advent of the Internet probably has proved the demise of the printed literary magazine.

But whether we lasted or not, we were there, and I'm as proud of *Dialog* as I am of *Phosphene*, and for the same reason— we published some darn good stuff. The best of it is in this collection except for the interviews with writers, which have been published in a separate volume along with profiles of other Texas writers.*

So, here is *The Best of Dialog* to give you an idea of what was going on in those days when Houston's Montrose Area was hip instead of upscale, and Shipley's ruled the night.

* Published in *Drifts: Texas Writers—Interviews and Profiles*, compiled and edited by Christopher Dow

POETRY

JAMES BETTISON

AFTER . . . DINNER . . . THOUGHT . . .

In a minute
I would have
Eaten all the years.
To taste you
Only once.

R. T. Castleberry

Sketch for Mourning

I do not sit to rest
But dream and drink this sweet, Sunday wine
As August moves to September
And the summer women turn their faces to fall's cool edge.
In the high haze of morning heat
I stand in the doorway
And watch the brown curl and fall of leaves
      on cracked and pebbled walkways,
        on stairways of creaking wood or marble.
I lean to lift my drink from the stoop
And walk out to sit in the cool, dry smell of bamboo and brick.

I have people to mourn.
And I will do it with sweet, dark liquor,
Within the silence of this stained glass bar,
The quiet between the call and the response of a Motow oldies
    hit.
As I walk to stand unsteady at the railing
The white and grey of ice turns
To the swift symphony of old radio songs and the dances of
    skaters,
To the blast and shriek of teen-agers in play.
As I stand in the cool, half shadows of fall
Or walk, to stumble in confusion,
I can hear the oily strain and click of a builder's crane,
The cries of men as they work in concrete dust or mud.
I hear the laughter fade as the summer women tremble and
    move home.
I have people to mourn.

Robert Dante

Lessons in Charm

with some few precious possessions, I treasure too
our Scorpions, in each tail
a self-indulgence
like a black leather rose, rising
from a red bible,
red as lips which kiss arteries,
smooth as thumbs along lapels,
hammers of steel ringing
against evening's elemental colors, as we
pause to catch our breaths
between ticket stubs—

we try to remember what day it is,
which city we're in, Teasingly—
"The South ain't what it was," I sigh;
"It never was," you say.

The Persistence of Memory

Sunlight billows through
the sea in unanswered worlds
around us—

flowers blossom in my fingers,
down your shoulders and breasts,
unfurling whorls of light along
the singing nerves
inside my sky-brown arms

limbs of coiling smoke, we weave
unloomed imaginations—
we breathe . . .

Direct communication between species
is already a fact,
beyond our merely beating on those barriers
between us—the wolf and human
will howl new poems
into each other's bones—

we will engrave the trembling planets
with a common footprint
and gaze out at new Zodiacs
through a single eye . . .

We pull ourselves shimmering
up, toward the surface of sleep—
the tentacles inside my chest
fly on a phosphorescent current,
hungry for more

CLAIRE DONOHUE-KOROLENKO

PECAN DAY

I have the pecans in the blue cooking pot
Near the tree they owned, up to now
And in the sun, they shine

Away from the water spouts
Where the rain runs,
And dark brown jungle tears fall beside our window

Plunking, one by one, down through the Texas sun
The pecans hide, in the rain bursts
Away in the weed-grass snarled at my feet

In rhythm, they rattle on the roof
The rain rustles past on by to farther up north
A chameleon zigzags through puddle danger zones, all
As you sleep, in your room, summertime warm,
Hearing the pecans fall in your dreams.

CHRISTOPHER DOW

FALL FLIES

Black speck on the wall—
Closer—Fly. Fat fly.
Buzz from the left, at the window
To sunlight and green early fall.
Three fat early fall flies.
With no malice, I
Shake a finger in the air
One inch over the wall-bound one.
Don't fly, I say in my mind. Just
Let me shake my finger at you.
It does not fly. I shake.
I turn to those others,
Silhouetted against nature,
All fat and easy to squash.
One crouches, the next buzzes
A bit in the air, the third
Walks up the left window molding,
Buzzing, under a shimmering thread.
Another thread. Another. Spiderweb.
My eyes range up past the crawling fly,
To the upper corner of the window.
Over the body of a fly, a spider
Hunches. The fly is fresh and fat.
The spider touches and sucks.
Fat fly. The others buzz
In sporadic bursts against the window.

The one on the wall lobs itself
Through the air to the glass,
Thumping a landing on that surface.
The world a movie at its feet, it waits
In early fall's dappled warmth,
A fat fly with other fat flies,
Waiting for the freedom of night,
When bright panes do not
Mesmerize with illusions of escape,
When cool drafts lend
A ride to winged creatures
Through a world of darkness
And no transparent barriers.

Lisa Howell Fenton

After Reading Ayn Rand

Rivet by rivet
I balance between
Blueprint and construction, idea
And Action, stillness and

Motion

I am the builder
The building
Rising, rising
From dust, sweat and singing
At noon

Girder by girder
Lace of my circuitry
Elevated speed.   Perfect flight

A button pushed
I transmit light
Compete with the stars
By day the sun answers
My blue glass

Girder by girder
Atoms forged Building
This grandeur climbs the sky
A massive spire
            Pain, adversity
Only passing through fire
Iron ore to steel

Shining steel
For my purpose
Beauty that cannot be violated
Panoramas of distance
Shivering height
Claimed as mine, mine
Each moment: An invention

I stand
With the purity of creation
Above your city

You cannot touch me now

Lisa Goodman

Sitting on a Couch with an Absent Jazzman
(Dedicated to Art Pepper)

When Pepper played beware of sorrow—
catch you tapping with surprise
He blew a life found locked in sound
he sang the time go by.

A mystery of mind in Art
caged behind a note
> he wrote on white walls with his nails he
> scratched on a script of sax-in-smoke hot-
> licked the cell where he laid it all to life.

When Pepper played from way down under,
touching bottoms not perceived
under covers tight-shade-curtains
red-chinz flowered fifties-chic

women turned their hats in wonder
scotch-numbed throats like ice he slid,
fingered parts your mama said no
not to cry in public.

> I sit on blue and nod agreements,
> seeing what I used to hear
> fifteen years found him the freedom
> run me backwards this place spent,
> scared the moods will send me screaming

of attempted explanations lie
about the man now cold; so
hot-stopped, jammed-packed, now survives
the late-night talkshow jazzed-up jives
of men who did not know his pride.
(I cannot claim I did.)

Sweat made sweet
the vibrant night
sound like baby-bottom smell
he played the truth with storm behind it
soothing me with lullabies in lies
the velvet-voiced man says
"no one can still the mystery of Art."

NINA HAAS

IMPATIENCE

Perhaps other old people are better . . .
But do not depend on me!
That breathless impatience,
So charming in youth,
—Salero, you called it,
A spoon-full of fire—
Has wilted into a course
Too impatient to care,
To water, to tend,
Even the flowers . . .
My poor fuchsias survive
On a sliver of conscience.

Kristin Higgins

The Sculptor Manque

How easy it would have been
for your tongue of highly polished silver
with the finest edges
to smooth and shape me
into your favorite pattern.

How easy
had I never learned to hone myself
with my own tools
had I not seen
that your favorite pattern left no room for mine
and that your tongue
was no tool of love.

LYN LIFSHIN

MY SISTER'S DIARIES

spread out in the dark
room of the house
where sleet bent
pines are dripping,
diaries like shells
a blood sun catches
glass turned ruby and
cranberry in altered
light. Her today, a
net of holes. But
these leather books
with their spines
cracking like debris
from a wrecked ship
burning to surface
stud the colorless
crystalline haze
the way a field of
jonquils push
thru snow

VIRGINIA LONG

REMEMBERED FRAGRANCE

Delicate and sweet as Chinese
wind chimes to the ear, remembered
fragrance can conjure those images
long lost to time. . .

Jasmine adrift on night wind —
the way magnolia hangs, heavy
in the grey dawn, or from dark
closets, faint and haunting, a hint
of cedar, sandalwood or rose.

A woman brushes near, and drifts
of perfumed air stir sharp fragments
of youth's old longings —
that crushed gardenia on a prom dress,
love notes sprouting violets,
and oh! those walks in autumn's mist.

Wet leaves spreading a sponge underfoot,
earth-mold pungent in the cool damp —
illusive now her beauty, faded
by years, but the scent she wore
                    remembered forever.

PHILLIP LOPATE

STRAIGHT MAN

Dear Warren, I often think about that night
you took me to an all-male gathering
for someone in the City Ballet corps.
A small brownstone apartment; we got jammed
against the kitchen table with the wine,
and some corpulent, red-faced, oily queen
accosted you with his belligerent lust:
"*Well!* Where have *you* been hiding out?" he screamed,
and dove his hand down-shirt, squeezing your chest.
You winced, still looking tolerant and amused.
Yes you were quite the favorite that night,
as well you should have been, my handsome friend.
Discouraging no one, giving none consent,
the perfect coquette, while I stood by your side
for safety's sake, as though your newest date;
I must have been the only straight man there.

But then I went into the living room
and gave you time to operate alone.
Besides, I was afraid to stick around
and see you in too-vivid an embrace—
collecting memories which might disturb
the fragile balance of our new friendship.
The men inside were making out or cruising;
that didn't faze me, they were not my friends.
What hurt, however, was the eye-contact,
first greedy, then disgusted when they saw
I didn't know the code. They looked *through* me,
as if to say, "You don't belong with us."
I sensed hostility—or at least chagrin

at my blocking their visual line of fire—
and circled, finding nowhere safe to stand.

Then Dave, your critic friend, came up to me
in kindness, and we started talking films.
He told me he'd been reading Noel Burch;
Burch claimed most Westerners misread Japanese films,
they thought they understood the little cues
but their ethnocentrism deluded them,
all part of bourgeois–humanist hegemony. . . .
His words kept getting more abstract, the more
I saw the party heating up around us.
A moment's paranoia made me think
he was insinuating a connection:
Just as the Japanese codes eluded me,
so did I misperceive the patterns here.

I kept insisting it was possible
for a round-eye like me to "get" Ozu.
The argument went drily circular
but I clung to it, having nothing else,
til from the corner of my eye I caught
your leather jacket and red flannel shirt.
You whispered in my ear: "*Nu?* Had enough?"
"I'm ready to go," I said, and seized your sleeve.
You laughingly apologized on the stairs:
"What an obnoxious party. If I'd known
such boring assholes would be there, you can
believe I'd never have invited you!"

We walked up Broadway to the subway stop.
I wanted to complain to you how strained
the whole experience had been for me,

how real the gulf
between men of your preference and mine.
We were like ancient enemies who posed
threats to each other by our being,
mocking the turn where each had gone his way.
how could I trust you—or you me?—
beyond formal exchange of the latest tastes.
Why had you put me through this nightmarish masquerade?

Yet even as I framed the words, I sensed
the party hadn't been that strange.
I was exaggerating the sensual shock
to alienate myself from what had been
as unoutrageous as my shadow, as
the doctor's question put at seventeen:
"What are you most afraid of? Speak, first thought—!"
"That I'd become a homosexual."
So I didn't, though I might have, and you did.
Friends live the lives we don't have time for,
or temperament, or talent. Forgive me if
I still seem both repelled and envious:
a part of me may never understand.

JOHN LUNSTROTH

UNTITLED

Against the line usually seen
as the horizon is a woman.
Enthralled by the sun, the hot
celestial body, she deserted
a dust covered plain and her people.

In robes she walked, when the moon was bright
as fire, towards the elaborate ocean. She passed,
suspended in desire, from anonymous rooms,
through the megaliths of modern man;
what history had etched beauty in her eyes,
what religion had formed childhood
so carefully in her body.

I was fishing that night, throwing time
after time my line through the waves,
when I saw her step from the sea wall
into the sand, I saw her procession
to the foamy saltwater, I saw the first
of ten sacraments in the wine-dark
sea, before she consummated devotion
in the burning swell of the dawn.

No longer with interest do I see Wisdom
define the horizon, no longer am I
enthralled with his strength as his fingers
pry chaste Night from her rooms.

Orson T. Maquelani

On a Lover's Bridge to Reality

Words more smooth than
the street-side blade:
like a hoodlum you still leave me
bleeding

way past needing
and again I hear your price.

The bridge is a terrible thing to cross

wishing not knowing
but wishing

Truth between your lies.
Still now
your words not even I

can toss.

Elizabeth McBride

The Atoll

When the tide was low
and the ocean water flowed
from the still lagoon and into the sea,

I wanted to walk out
on the crest of the coral ring
and circle the reef,

past the shallow pools
where spiny lobsters feed,
crawling at night from ocean side to lagoon.

One day I went so far
I saw the shark's fin slitting a line
through the dark water toward me.

I could barely hear my mother's voice
calling, barely see my father standing,
still, on the shore.

KWAJALEIN

When I was a child,
my father took me to live
on an island.
Day after day the light
fell through the window
and into my bedroom
and day after day I woke
and ran to the sea.
There with my feet deep in the sand
I looked across from the beach
to the coral reef.
It appears even more clear
to me now than then,
the sky spread around
the rim of the atoll,
and the sun bright in the sky
and again in the sea.
When I imagine that child,
my eyes are green as the shallow
lagoon and my skin as smooth
as the underside of a palm
leaf. I can almost touch her,
almost feel her hair,
long and straight down my back
as a memory.

SHELLS

That year, I fed the tiger-striped cat
my father loved, the one
that howled all night from the water tower
and slept all day beside the back steps
guarding the shells.

Buried there in the sand, they
yielded their meat to the ants.
Then my father, satisfied, dug them up
and soaked them in acid until
their surfaces were rippled glass.

When in my play at the edge of the water
I discovered shells still
full of flesh and smelling of the sea,
I took them to the steps—
my prayers, my offerings.

Robin McCorquodale

Andres Segovia, We Want to Show You Our Henry Moore

1

Andres Segovia,
we want to show you our Henry Moore.
Mr. Moore told us where to place it and then he said:
"On the thirty-first of October,
in the year, one thousand nine hundred and seventy nine,
on the night that Houston commemorates the return of all
     souls
with a Moonlight Bicycle Ramble,
my sculpture will be here placed."

I replied,
"Mr. Moore, on the thirty-first
the faithful will fall onto bronze
believers will clasp hands, shake hands and give the holy kiss,
steaming up the metal arches.
Cyclists will make twenty miles look like two or one,
but I shall look where you have adjusted the curve
and shall begin to worship."

2

Maestro Segovia,
Houston is my home and Valladolid is yours,
but would you play something British?

On this knoll, Allen Parkway, beside Buffalo Bayou's clay shores,
we have placed "Spindle Piece." Play:
> Thomas Tallis
> Benjamin Britten
> Frederick Handel
> Ralph Vaughan Williams
> for Henry Moore.

THE PROMISE

Clover created waves for cattle to stand in.

The clover for the girl to walk in
   ripples:
     on a lake, like a lake
       created more swells for that girl and grackles and crows
         to fly through and disappear in;
           for sandals to sink into,
             one bee now a dozen dive into blossoms,
               like seagulls diving into surf
                 come out with fish.

The clover backed off in
surges of green,
a pond to prance into on high-heeled sandals
for these shoes to sink
for bees to accumulate and buzz,
sunshine, low-flying clouds, hard as rocks
the clover fell sideways heavy on its 4th leaf,
therefore, most remarkable of plants
undulating green for straw birds and pipers,
cattle to drown in, to melt under hoofs
with insects to shout in their
humdrumming ears; shining cows
the girl strokes
makes much over, touches and they
ring their bells;
for sandals to hurry past,
to sink into green when the man
held the barbed-wire fence far enough apart,

caught his shirt, cursed, smiled, walked into clover waves toward
her.

Billows in clover,
   floating on it
     swelling in green: to
       separate two lines of barbed wire
         incorporate bees in the picture
          and the girl's face (she smiles)
          in exposure to wind and sun
            not five yards away; while the
              clover backs off:
                sinks, rises,
                  into blushing
                    when the man as a man
takes
her hand
flowers are stars
really.
It is the
wind which
rocks the clover;

slips on the ring
over her finger, ripples
the green wind in clover
bees are a voice of golden families;
the sky, yes blue, another sea:
clouds swell, billow;
when the man lifted the barbed-wire
put one foot on the barbed wire, waded out to the girl in green;
rippling for boots to plunge into,

clover, his knee,
fell over the fourth leaf, the third
so on one knee; his third and fourth wish, a clover:
the day of exquisite luck, the green
he handed her a four-leaf one
the ring and his promise.

JOAN McNEARNEY

AN EXECUTIVE

showed me in
in this dream
i, shy
as an orphan

her charming face
through sewing room
viewing cabinets
bolts of silk
tactical prints
her life in threads
swatches impressive
floral

discerning glances
make me hurry
out the rear
but she invited
me only to see
her material things
& feel them
unattainable

all handsome houses
have well guarded gardens
lush chrysanthemums
smothering me
dog-faced.

D. MEEKS

BING CHERRIES, PURPLE PLUMS

Anatomy, Pathology, this building reeks of death.

Long past the sudden reaching for breath,
The astonished grunt or surprising sticky warmth
They lie, a hand, a foot, a gleaming eye
Dreaming within its clever fringe of lash.

The dark comes on so early now.
We skitter across the parking lots
Keeping our thighs together,
Holding ourselves with our own arms
In damp November chill.
We are so frail.

I need summery arms, sure and alive,
The scent of Sea and Ski,
Your mouth, what it must have,
Your voice, that wordless growl.
The twist of urgency, your face
Hard against my brow.

Summer will come, oh, say it will
With those heaped stands beside summer roads
Gleaming cherries, mounds of grapes, purple plums
All the tight-skinned fruit that bursts and runs
And we will have sun and sun and Queen Anne's lace
And violins and metal drums

And we will not remember
This dank, basement November scent
Down where the air is bad.

Formaldehyde, formaldehyde, when did these lungs know breath?
Pathology, Anatomy, these pickles stink of death.

SEACHANGE

Moist and breathy, sticky-handed, patting
The wind swung around, last night.
The porchscreens are disconsolate.
The Gulf breathes thicker air and gives off mist.
The cutweeds sway and list and sibilantly break
Beneath this strange assault.

Ah, hell.
We were so strong
Pajamas inside our jeans
All winter long, cursing this broken house
Bulwarked against the north.

But who could fight off this pitiless unknowing?
This incessant, soft demand?

Damp and busy
Persistent as a two-year-old
The wind swung around in the false dawn, today.

The Gulf breathes heavily. The house
Leans, groaning, into the north.

Vassar Miller

Fear

Fear
no gentleman with
the stink of his sweat
and flatulent guts,
not pausing to dry
his boots on the mat
of a metaphor,
he tramples the nerves,
squats down in the mind,
picking the bones of
courage and honor.

A Rage for Order for Rose

From my back porch I'm watching God's housekeeping
And think you wouldn't want Him in your house:
No Lordy! Like them mens, no good at sweeping,
And look, just will you, all those leaves fly loose!
That great big broom God makes those old fall winds with
Like He ain't thought about nobody's yard.
Those clouds! Not fit to dry your hands with,
No wonder you could slap a tree trunk hard!
And, say, don't tell you how God wastes some comet,
And spends a million years on one amoeba
When you could, —Lord, have mercy ain't no limit—
You go and close your window—just how He be.
And now, be-hold! God gets Hisself a few
Dobabs all throwed around
                              and dear like you.

SLEEP

walked off and left me
just like any no-good man.
He left my thoughts,
so many little bare-assed kids
gawking at one another
up in my attic,
this creaky old house full of night noises.

You ever see that bastard,
you tell him he won't find a love
good as mine.

WHAT REALLY HAPPENS

We are the cat who worries time away,
tossing it hither, *thunk,* and thither, *thwack,*
tail twitching, while between its paws its prey
flops back and forth and back
until the feline master of the house,
with time, poor thing routinely mauled to sweeten
monotony, forgets that time's the mouse
that kills in being eaten.

Harryette Mullen

A Brand of Love

I want her superstitious about me,
so she put me on like an amulet—
never take me off.

I want to pierce her like a hot needle
that hurts only for a second.
I want to be the gold
she hang in her earlobe,
swinging out to touch her cheekbone
when she laugh
or when she shake her head.

Want her wearing my smell like perfume.
My smell on her body
like a "No Trespassing" sign.

I want to touch her with fire
from the burning bush
so she'll always feel my fingers
hot on her skin.

Marie Ponsot

Metro Bus

1. We Take What We Can

Midnight, winter, corner of Elgin & Main,
men I'm afraid of; so far I've been wrong.
All four lurch and lean; a fifth snores in a stain
of his own liquids. I know I can't belong
at this bus-stop at this time of night.
All five ignore me as I look alert,
pace briskly from edge to edge of pooled streetlight.
Do they know/ I don't/ if the drunk fifth is hurt
& if he is, what to do. Here an hour,
no phone, not one walker, just rush-rush cars,
stubbornly we six exert no power,
risk no looks. Waiting is who we are.

Bus at last. My relief smiles its trust.
The bus driver looks at me with pained disgust.

2. We Envision What We Can

August. After noon. Heat. Heat endured like fate
slows us, stuns. Hair curls. Eyes sting. The heat lasts
till 4 AM; the let-up lasts till 8,
when walkers quit. Only cars move fast.

My bus-stop neighbor gasps and fans. She prefers
to clean house for señoras who don't mind
her grandbaby coming to work with her

in conditioned air, but they're hard to find.
Things will be better for the Rosa baby
born in Texas: Americana citizen,
no problema, job, car, high-school maybe.
Envisioned, Rosa smiles & smiles again.

I blink to find that old wild dream alive.
Rosa invites her grandma out to drive.

MUSEUM

1. For a Christmas Visitor

The fountained garden of the Museum
of Art becomes you in your clarity.
I often breakfast here. I like to come,
down from the medieval gallery
& its little ivories that strike me dumb,
to this water-music. Today I see
that what was lacking was your company . . .
the vivid child in you whom you summon
to scout out & open the lost famous gate
of the world of wishes. In you run
& with a rush of words leave fantasy
for forecast: "This wish is good. I choose this one."
Selves drawn from self, you plan work you define;
you shine, good woman; garden & fountain shine.

2. A Century of Modern Sculpture

On the white wall: 4 bronze-black backs—Matisse
trying to muscle shoulder into arm;
up the steps: reason sports in a Calder piece;
a Dave Smith fusses; Benglis holds out gilt charm;
an eggsmash scrambles the post-modern soul.

I always make the same mistake. I come
toward sculpture to find, beyond my control,
some grail, some sign, hand-made, eloquently dumb,

set out for me to walk around & around
amazed as I listen & hear it hum.
It can happen. It happens, look, there by the door,
a stone girl proposes simple hands, her whole
body simple like the cup I came here for:
firm light lasts on her, the Flore of Maillol.

PATTIANN ROGERS

THE MYTH OF THE FIELDS

> . . . into his gates with
> thanksgiving and into his
> courts with praise . . .

The bluet blossoms lie thin and transparent
As petal-shaped slivers of a cold sky fastened
To the earth. The seedhead of a dawn, as icy wheat,
Brushes the sun-touched withers of the rising colt.
And the pony-scented sun rises, spilling flashing seeds
Of ice above the deeply buried petals of a black sky.

The court of god is the presence
Of this myth in the field, a court entered
By particles of thanksgiving discovered as light
Inside the quiver of the pony's haunch, inside the thin
Fire of ice cracking across the columned grasses.

And the kingdom of the field is the sheathed
And hooved, the rooted and earth-tight myth
Of god, the traceable electrons of that myth existing
As opening gate of potential light found and witnessed
Inside the intimate body of bluet, inside
The failing sound of the pony's call.

This point of praise for the sunsheathed stem
And broken-bladed frost is, in fact, half particle,
Half cresting effluence of illumination itself.

The sight seen through the open gates
Of the seeded bluets, the frozen blades

And icy myth of the sun, the shining shoulders
And frosted mane of god, all must enter into being,
Solely and at once, through the recognized form
Of their inseparable praises.

A SEQUENCE OF CIRCUMSTANCES

Inside a real forest of blue ash, blue beech,
Speckled alder and ward willow, there is an imaginary
Lake bordered by greenbriar and honeysuckle,
By frogbit, lily and rushes of waterweed.

On that imaginary lake there is a real vision
Of two lovers drifting alone in the dusk
Beside the tangled banks of dark forest, lovers
Whispering together as they lie side by side
In the bow of the boat.

Within this real vision the woman makes imaginary
Trails across the surface of the moon
On the lake as if she actually explored the dust
Of that light by the tip of her finger moving
Over the water's white craters and their peaks.
By the imaginary trails her finger makes there,
The real moon on any real night is not known
And witnessed hereafter to be
Forever marked by fable.

And when her lover first bends to kiss her breast
In the dusk, moving his lips slowly across the dark
Of her nipple exactly as if he were a fable
Discovering the soft, hidden surface of some unmarked
Moon, there is a recognition of motion rising

In the mind, a motion reminiscent itself of dusk-scented
Lake water rocking slowly like a cherishing breath
Slowly discovering an imaginary sky, a real motion
Of recognition which could never have existed at all
Through any sequence of circumstances
Other than these.

Remembering the Imagination:
A Love Letter

Can you imagine remembering the rain, less than rain,
Yesterday morning, almost a stationary mist,
Imperturbable and weightless, a mist remembering
To exist in those places where nothing else
Was imagining itself to exist at that moment?

I remember myself imagining the spun moisture
Arching inside the inner-surface fuzz
Of every pre-dawn leaf and the glint of the condensation
On the outer surface of each of those dark green
Memorable leaves. I can imagine the fog
Completely filling the oak tree with more spaces
Than it could ever remember having possessed before.

And I remember the pine tree, maintained and encased
Inside the mist, holding one clear precipitate drop
Poised at the pinnacle of each of its sharp edges,
As if the tree had suddenly imagined in glass
Those precise points at which it had ceased forever
To remember its identity.

Can you imagine the clear golden horses existing
Inside and outside the fog, never remembering to imagine
Their perimeters, leaving themselves thus vulnerable
To that indefinite mist moving at will in and out
Of their rib bones and flanks, their fetlocks and withers?
The fog, moving in and out of the gold lenses

Of their disappearing eyes, could easily carry
In either direction whatever vision the horses
Might choose to imagine themselves remembering.

Imagine the fog, appearing, if the horses
Remember it simultaneously, as smoke blown from their nostrils,
Or appearing, if the horses imagine it simultaneously,
As billows of pale surf rolling over their disintegrating
Hooves. If the horses should emerge snorting
And rearing on the surface once more, imagine yourself shouting
To them before they sing again, "Remember, remember
To imagine the total gold boundaries of your possible existence."
Outside the imagination, no one had ever been able to remember
Anything of gold horses which have forgotten themselves.

At the distance from which you read this,
Try to imagine an invisible fog filling like light
More spaces between us than we might remember exist, ignoring
Those perimeters we have chosen to forget, an indefinite light
Moving freely from eye to eye, easily carrying the vision
Of everything I might wish to imagine that you remember
Of my existence at this moment.

JACQUELINE SIMON

THE BILOXI SHRIMPER CONFESSES TO HIS MONSIGNOR

The Gulf doesn't hold so much:
where my grandfather used to get 50, 75 barrels a day,
I bring in 15 pounds.
Boats now are bigger, too, more efficient.
It doesn't take so many.
Yesterday there were so many boats
you could barely see the horizon.
We drag our nets east and west,
they go any way they please!
They cut across our fields, one cut across my bow.
When a sensible man comes in from squalls and lightning,
they stay out, all day, all night.
At the Blessing of the Fleet, where were they?
Already at work. But they're Catholics, too.
Christ says, Make peace among you.
But Christ would have said
you don't make peace
by running across your brother's field.
Now both sides go armed: tensions run high.
It's no way to live.

The Monsignor Replies to the Shrimper

They're out there on the water
because it's the only place they have.
Their trawlers carry families, wives, and babies.
They'll learn your laws and customs:
you think they want more violence?
Though I know they have their rifles, too.
Give them time, let them make their way.
The Gulf belongs to all the people—
now they're the people, too.
You want more shrimp in your double riggers;
you've got a thirty thousand dollar boat,
two thousand worth of nets.
Today you made four hundred
and the profit wasn't clear.
Nguyen Cao Ky gave them forty thousand, more,
to buy their boats.
He'll be looking for something in return.
That's at the problem's core, brother.
It isn't only the Vietnamese.
It's in the human heart.
The Gulf doesn't hold so much.

Sidney Wade

French Lilacs

The earth by now has given up its claw-toothed crocus,
its first born. Still, in shadows,
snow lingers like the smell of old leaves.
The soil has been expanded and torn,
then resettled by the force of the sun.
This morning is dark.
The wind blows and the air is heavy with rain.
The pomegranate heads of the lilacs toss,
glance off one another, bruises among the leaves.
I saved the rose you once gave me.
In its narrow box it aged to the color of dried blood.
Now I stand beneath these sudden flowers
and remember how we rose in those mornings,
light filling our eyes.

Two Leaves

It is barely spring, and I stand here
in the warming sun, hoping that God
will give me a vision, or children,
preferably both. I can see the balanced-
out leaves of last year's poplars and hear
their delicate rattle. The buds of the shade
trees swell, tighten, and shine when
snow still lies heavily on their branches.
I think of death, of course. The snow,
though deep yet, is dying in its own way—
giving itself up to swollen currents,
brilliance in the sun, somehow joyous
in this transformation. I am alone
by chance, not by nature, and dismayed
at this condition. My feet are cold. Sense
withdraws as the blood shuts down. Just
as I move to head back home I hear
the chirr of the cardinal. Its blood-
red body beats into the light when
it bursts from the trees—the branches
discard wet snow and the bird disappears
into the face of the sun which floods
this white ground with indifference,
and I am warmed to the bone by this circumstance.

CHRISTOPHER WOODS

TENNESSEE

Outside Pigeon Forge, the highway mists
In dying dusk.
My hands and eyes aching, I pull to the side
To rest, and if not,
Then to dream this all again, in sequence.
Walking through the underbrush,
Smoky Mountain air begs me to enter the past.
In my jacket I carry arrowheads,
Ones you left.
You left them, not for me, just left them.
A person leaves hints of what he was.
Arrowheads, cool and sharp, are all I have of you.
I must have been clouds, then, when you lived.
Dressed in flannels, you were geiger-counting the hills,
To take Tennessee if you could,
As it has always been in family memory.
Your journeys were holy travels, personal crusades.
Brother in time, we are tantamount to seasons
Of unbroken circles.
It all depends where and how time places itself.
Grandfather, I never even met you.
Time is dead but for the living,
So hot to annihilate time
And get to know ourselves outside the concept
Intrigues me.

As for you, old man, this vision will last,
Flickering in photographic haze.
Do you know, no matter how I hold my head,
Mine is still a neanderthal walk,
Clutching these arrowheads in Tennessee?

FICTION

MARIE DYBALA

A ROSE FOR ANNA

WHAT HAD HURT THE MOST was the loss of Anna. Joseph slumped into his hard, wooden chair. The shirt that once fit him well sagged at the shoulders and his right sleeve dropped limply at his side. Thin strands of white hair lay on his head. The house he built had changed little over the years other than the addition, finally, of the telephone, which rarely rang. The same dusty pictures covered the walls in frames he had carved with careful hands years before. The young faces of his children smiled eagerly from the old photographs. He stared blankly at the weeds that had overtaken his vegetable garden. He sighed and shook his head. Occasional houses had sprung up on the horizon like mushrooms after a spring rain. He longed to look back into the setting sun with no obstacles to obscure his view. He hoped to hear Anna bustle in the kitchen and to touch the long black braid she wound in a ball on the back of her head every morning. But she only returned to him in his dreams.

His head tilted toward the right so he could watch his son's cattle graze in the pasture across the gravel road. He had to strain to find the small dark dots in the green haze. Why could he see the brown dot cows more clearly than the things he held in his hand, he wondered. He could no longer read the Czech newspaper, *Vestnik,* that lay before him on the coffee table. When relatives sent letters he had trouble opening them. At night before he slept, he could no longer even read the Bible. He remembered the epic letters he wrote to his family in Europe. And that journal he had kept with each year's profits and losses etched in its yellowed pages. Where was it now? His life eclipsed while he sat in the darkness and waited. Aquamarine eyes hid behind heavy lids.

"Let's see what brother George has to say," Mary would announce with a pile of mail scattered on her aproned lap. But he was asleep before she finished the letter.

His life was like a dream now. He no longer felt contained in his body. At times, he stretched like a spider web in a dark corner. Then he drifted like a cloud of vapor across time and space. He would find himself in Kromeriz, Czechoslovakia, where he was born. He walked down the dirt path and saw his father in the back yard heave an ax over his shoulder to split logs. He smelled the honeysuckle that grew on the vine beside him and saw the delicate flowers that his mother cared for like her own children. The bluest of blue humming birds, a promiscuous lover, flitted from one flower to the next. The rise and fall of his mother's voice echoed in song through the open window where two loaves of bread rose and waited to be baked.

More often, he returned to his new life in America. He remembered how his knuckles pounded his uncle's door the night they met for the first time. He had taken a train from Galveston and arrived in Cameron earlier than expected. His English was awkward, and he walked through the dark streets with his heavy trunk pressing into his back until he found a man who spoke Czech. He followed his directions and walked the two miles to his uncle's farm. He bowed his head and trudged down the unfamiliar road. He tried to imagine what it would look like in the sunlight. His mind filled with apprehension. The unusually flat land made him feel like an intruder in a stranger's house. The cold wind slapped his face and burned his eyes.

Sounds brought him back to the blue wall. Mary bustled about the room. She swept the floor and gathered the newspapers. "We will have a visitor, your grand-daughter, Marenka," she urged in Czech. He had not spoken to anyone but Mary in weeks. His son John had visited several times, but he always slept and missed him. So he forgot what Mary fussed about and faded away into his dream world.

He saw himself awaken in the house across the street that now had its windows boarded and its floor rotted. The image of his first farm in Texas, a large house with smoke unfurling out the chimney made him smile. He remembered the yard filled with people who drank beer and ate barbecue the day he was married. The large empty rooms felt extravagant when he lived there alone. In the mornings, his only companions were a chorus of birds on his rooftop. After he kindled the fire in the stove, he grabbed his jacket and hurried out to the barn. The sun, a cold and distant friend just above the horizon, illuminated the earth with a pale, red glow. He opened the long, wooden gate and let the cattle out to graze.

On Sundays, he could take the time to walk to the forest of baby pine trees he had planted and measure how tall they had grown. On this particular Sunday, after breakfast, he gazed into the mirror and combed the thick crop of brown hair with more than the usual attention. He lathered his face and carefully scraped the short stubble from his cheeks and chin. He looked pleased into his deep, blue eyes, but was distracted by the tangle of his eyebrows. He damped his fingers in the steaming water and smoothed the protruding hairs. He even trimmed his mustache. He dressed for church in his finest blue suit, tipped his hat to the right, straightened his tie, and walked onto the front porch where he waited. It was a cold winter morning, and a blanket of frost still glistened in the fields, but the fierce sunlight quickly dissolved its lacework. Soon, he could see her long, black hair that flowed from under her scarfed head and danced around her bundled body. At the perfect moment, he walked onto the road with his prayer book in his left hand. He slowed his pace until he heard her footsteps behind him. With a gentle turn, he met her blue eyes and smiled into them for the first time.

He extended his right hand. "Good morning, my name is Joseph, may I walk you into town?" She looked down, and he continued. "I noticed you in church last Sunday. We must be neighbors." She remained silent. He nervously clasped his damp palms and tried to carry on a conversation, but she would not answer him. He was sure she despised him and tried to think of a graceful way to disguise his chagrin. Then, he mentioned he lived alone and his family was in Czechoslovakia. Her eyes lit up and she spoke in soft, Czech words.

"I, too, am from Czechoslovakia. My name is Anna." She glanced into his eyes to see that he understood, then continued. "My family just moved here a few weeks ago and my English is not good. I was too embarrassed to try to speak to you. I'm so glad you speak Czech." She laughed. Joseph's heart pounded when she held his arm and allowed him to escort her to and from church. The following Sunday, he met her again and offered her a red rose, moist with dew drops, from his garden.

The next week was unbearable for him. The days dragged and a storm raged that prevented him from working in the fields. He sat on the porch and grimaced each day. His eyes searched the road to the east as if he expected Anna's tall slender body to appear. In frustration, he went to his garage where he busied himself for hours. In the work area, he found his tools and an old sheet of metal that he began to carve and shape. He sat beside his tractor and looked around to make certain everything was in its proper place. The dirt floor was smooth and dustless despite the rain outside. Onion and garlic dangled on ropes above his head. He painted the petals he had wrought bright red and yellow. He planned when and how he would present them to Anna this next Sunday instead of the customary red rose. After church, he decided to take her on a tour of the farm. When he showed her his tractor and work room, he would give her the flowers and invite her to a dance the following Saturday. His blood surged with a new sensation while he gazed out the window at the falling rain. He sat content with his pipe and blew smoke rings into the clearing sky.

A hand gripped his shoulder and rocked him forward to the present. His eyes watered, and in the haze, he discerned two figures. One leaned over his shoulder and felt familiar as she shifted his pillows and helped to lift him in his chair. "I'm fine, don't worry with me, Mary," he muttered. Again he noticed the other figure who he thought resembled Anna. He saw her lips move and heard a mumble of words. He motioned for her to come closer and explained that he could not see well and that, without his right arm, he was not the strong man he used to be. In the light, he vaguely recognized his granddaughter, Marianne, whom Mary fondly called Marenka. She still looked like Anna, except that she dressed in such peculiar men's clothes; blue jeans and a long sleeved shirt.

"Hello, Grandfather, how do you feel today?"

He tried to smile at her, but his eyelids felt thick. She asked him many questions in English, and his eyes followed her movements around the room with great concentration. When he answered her, she always responded with an anxious look.

"Grandfather, I don't speak Czech, please tell me in English."

One of the questions hit a nerve that vibrated through his body. It echoed in the corridors of his memory.

"What was it like to come to America, Grandfather?"

He struggled to form sentences, but could only manage to say, "Kromeriz."

"What?"

"The *Koeln*," he uttered, then, "It was a cold wind." His eyes closed, and she sat beside him with his rough, wrinkled hand in hers.

He remembered when his hair was brown and wavy and his skin smooth and fair under a wide brimmed felt hat. He waved to his family at the train station and set out, alone, for Bremen, Germany, where he would board the ship, the *Koeln*. He rode all night on the train but had difficulty sleeping. He stared out the window at the blurred images that rushed past in shadows. Tears rolled down his cheeks. He pictured his mother in her bright, navy gingham dress—the one she wore on special occasions.

In the morning, he awoke early and watched the sun slowly rise over tall stalks of sugar cane. Soon they reached the port, and he clutched his suitcase and trudged across the town to the dock. He noticed many other young men already waiting there when he arrived. He even recognized one, John, whom he had met on the train the night before. Women in bonnets walked close behind their husbands, with children at their sides. Husbands checked in the baggage ceremoniously. Women said last farewells to the few relatives who stood with their hands over their foreheads shielding the sunlight. He smiled into the warm eyes of his fellow immigrants, and the ship churned. He felt lucky as he buttoned his jacket and a cool breeze whipped over the water. The town disappeared, and the ship drifted further out until all he could see was the church steeple. His attention shifted to the swells of the current that bobbed the ship up and down like a toy. His hands began to sweat, and he felt a chill. An older man to his right, whom he guessed to be thirty-five or forty, removed his hat and spoke as if he was addressing everyone in sight. "I don't know about the rest of you, but I'm going to Texas to drill for oil, and I've never felt better in my life. I'll buy a schooner of beer for everyone who makes it to Galveston with me. I wish I was your age again, young man."

"Thank you, sir. The name's Joseph Vira, and I'm pleased to meet you."

"Anton Bauer, and it's a pleasure to meet you. Where is your wife and family?"

"I'm only seventeen, and I'm traveling alone, but I will be going to Galveston, and although I don't usually drink, I'll take you up on that offer."

"Well, of course you will; we're going to a free country." Bauer smiled and patted Joseph on the back.

"I'll have to be going soon," he heard Marianne say. She pressed a glass of water to his lips, but he insisted on holding it. She had stopped her questioning and sat with her hand on his arm. Her touch awakened his heart and he felt a strong yearning to communicate. He wished she spoke Czech like Mary or that his English was better. He remembered the first time he met Anna and chuckled aloud.

Finally he spoke. "I want to visit Anna, but I'm too old and tired. Would you go for me?"

She squeezed his hand in hers.

"There is a rose bush by the porch. Bring her a red rose. It was her favorite flower." He added. His eyes closed.

Marianne kissed him good-bye. She carefully clipped one long stemmed blossom and embraced Aunt Mary.

When he awoke, an auburn cloud hung in the western sky and twilight settled in the room like an evening visitor. Alone, he sat in the darkness and watched the moon rise in the east.

BILLIE SUE MOSIMAN

WILD STRAWBERRIES

HIS CONSTANT HOPE WAS TO find a way to heal them. Was there a way? The vicious attack on their son had left them all three wounded.

He walked into the room where shades were drawn against sunlight. She always longed for the sun, but now she'd turned her back on it.

A portable box fan trembled on the floor and blew stale air from one side of the room to the other. Magazines littered the floor beside the bed, dog-eared, some of the pages ripped loose.

He looked deeper into the artificial twilight. A book unread but open face down on a table beside a mug of cold coffee. The ashtray overflowed with ground butts. This was her world and no one else's. He sighed heavily and moved toward her where she lay sprawled across the bed, legs akimbo, eyes fluttering in half sleep.

The bed creaked agonies as he sat on the side of the mattress. He put one arm across her diminutive waist where the white slip was bunched. She struggled into wakefulness, one hand groped across the sheet as if to tug on a vanishing dream.

"You shouldn't do this to yourself," he said softly. What he meant was she shouldn't do it to either of them. He ached to hold her, but knew caresses held no salvation. Touching brought recoil and anger. He understood this too and left her alone.

She rubbed her eyes with doubled fists and suddenly flung them out in outrage. Life was too raw and sleep so easy.

"I know I shouldn't do it," she admitted. "I'm scared to death. All I want is Jimmy home. Where is our Jimmy?"

He waited, the silence a stone great as the room. Shadows spun past the shades and warbled from the force of the fan.

Everything moved—out there. In here, the tone pinned them to the bed.

"Can I just talk? Does it matter if I don't make any sense?" she asked, her eyes avoiding his.

"It doesn't matter."

Had the flecks in the depths of her brown cocoa eyes always been so dark and troubled? She was slipping away, and he let her go. He had no choice.

"First of all we move back South. You get a job with the Forest Service as a . . .ranger or park tender or something, you know, like that. We can live in the woods, and they'll give us a house. We can move and begin again, start all over. There aren't any cars or trains or ambulances or city noise." She paused, listening to a siren. "No gangs, either. No people crowding us. It's quiet. Birds everywhere. Pine trees—God, I miss the pines . You don't know how I miss them. Anyway, there are trees drooping over the front of the house where we sit on hot nights, smelling tar oozing out. It's lovely and quiet. Are you listening?"

"Yes, of course. Go on."

"You do things like check the county roads or woods or the wild animals. You make sure there aren't any fires left burning or whatnot. But the best thing is, we're free. No phones or worry over bills or noise or air that breathes like plastic wrap. I can read, sew, or just sit, and it won't make any difference."

She was fast slipping. She sucked in her breath, and he imagined she could already smell the forest, the tar, the musky quiet. He waited patiently for her to continue. He'd heard it before, but sometimes he was in the role of a marina handyman, and they lived on the beach in Gulf Shores, Alabama, or he was a county deputy responsible for the welfare of an under-populated area in Georgia. Always there was hope of escape, a running away to deserts, mountain retreats, woods, especially woods. Civilization had caused her severe disorientation. The city had always baffled her. Fantasy was an urgent detour in times of stress. Jimmy's stabbing had completely annihilated her tolerance for city living.

Tears dropped onto her slip, spotting it gray. She brushed her lashes angrily, and her eyes cleared.

"That would be nice, wouldn't it?" she asked. He nodded his assurance that, yes, her dreams were indeed nice dreams. They always were.

"A man has his choice about how he lives, doesn't he?" she asked. "We aren't cattle, are we, waiting for slaughter?"

He winced at the word at the same moment she did. He shifted his weight and struggled to right one ankle that had fallen asleep. It tingled, but he kept his expression bland, a baked custard face.

Creature of effortless days, he thought, as she fingered the sheet, thinking. Her imagination overblown by books. A romanticist caught in an age of realism.

But I love her. This is my fate to love her.

"You could do it, honey," she said, picking up the broken thread of her fantasy. "Some people live uncomplicated lives. I can see it now. Remember those parks we used to camp in when we were first married? They needed forestry people, attendants, somebody to watch over those places."

"I know."

"All right. I'll tell you about the house. It's wooden so the outside smells come through the cracks to reach us. There has to be a fireplace with a wide mantle. Lots of split logs piled neatly on the porch. It has to have a porch! And a swing, of course. Then the kitchen is important too. It faces the sunrise, so in the mornings we can eat by sunlight and supper is shadowy and cool. Not like here. Not like looking out the kitchen window on a chalky red building butted up against us and front windows that face the street. Did you know people, perfect strangers, crane their necks to look in on us? What do they want from me?"

He shook his head unhappily. Did people really spy on them like she said? He resisted an urge to glance at the shades.

"I'd have everything blue," she continued. "Blue curtains and white sashes and blue and white bedspreads. Hardwood floors. A big oval mirror hanging on the wall beside the mantle and vases and vases of wildflowers. They're the best, you know. Better than a hundred roses from the florist. Honeysuckle and dogwood branches in bloom. Goldenrod— but I used to sneeze around goldenrod. Violets and those wild orange irises that come out in June all along the roadsides. The house would be full of sweetness. At night, we'd count fireflies the way I did when I was a kid. If I could only hear a whippoorwill or a mockingbird. . . ."

Slipping. The South of her youth where sultry vines and bird calls forced her away from the whine of the traffic beyond the windows. The South. That country as strange and apart as if it was transplanted from the far edge of another galaxy. Something magic here, in the South. It suffused her blood with stories and tales, with memories, all of them hard-knuckled and sunburnt and smelling of dark loam and damp clay banks. She suffers an ancestral sickness. She left a trailing umbilical cord attached when she left the South, and it stretches across thousands of miles, its roots buried deep, deep in warm, baked soil. She is a prisoner, however unwilling, of her geography. He suspected this all along. She doesn't belong to him. She doesn't belong to Jimmy. The South had its claim first, and it's the strongest.

I don't understand.

He willed his thoughts to her, hoping for psychic intervention.

I don't understand, but sometimes when I'm still awake late at night, I wish I had your roots. I don't understand, but I wish I could dream your dreams and make them real. But the South, it's a spot on a map. It's only a place confined by a section of earth and climate. It's not even the same as it was twenty years ago when I took you away. Don't you know that? Time has ravaged the South, too. There have been cataclysmic changes while you weren't looking.

"There used to be a brook," she said, clasping hold of the dream by the coattail before it disappeared. "A little bit of water that ran behind my great aunt's house. I jumped across it when I was little, and it was big to me, almost too big to land on the other side without getting wet. The woods all around it. Steep sides, red clay. The water was clean, pure, cold and icy. Pale yellow sand shone from the bottom like fool's gold. I'd swing my arms in a great arc and jump. When I was hot and thirsty, I'd slide down to the water and lift the water in cupped hands. It was so good it makes my teeth ache to think of it.

"On the other side of the brook was a little kingdom. I'd find strawberries in the spring. They were the reddest things, like drops of blood spilled between saw-toothed leaves. I had to think real hard when I ate them. I had to think STRAWBERRIES, but when I got it right, they tasted as good as the big field strawberries. They tasted better! The weren't full of dust and grit and pithy centers. They were wild strawberries so they were made of dew and shade, the only stuff a little girl cares about.

"When I had my fill of them I put the sensitive plants to sleep. Of course, I didn't know what they were called then. They were just tiny, green willowy plants that magically went to sleep at my touch. I'd touch them all until the whole ground around me was sound asleep, dozing in the forest, and I was a fairy that had done this thing grown-ups couldn't do."

He was there. Tasting the wild berries, the cool, refreshing water, smelling the flowers, touching the sleeping plants. With great reluctance he drew himself up mentally. He had to. She was better, more stable, and they had to see Jimmy. One minute more. He could give her one minute. She pulled evenly and purposefully on her eyelashes.

"We have to go to the hospital."

"I know." Her fingers stopped their pacing across her eyes and she blinked at him, a wounded fawn guilty of nothing but a stumble towards survival. "I'll get ready."

He moved from her side to allow her room to stand. She pulled down the slip to cover milky thighs. She reached for a cigarette, hesitated, replaced it in the crumpled pack. He side-stepped as she brushed past him on the way to the bathroom. To feel busy, he picked up the discarded magazines, thumbing first this one, then that, glancing over the shining, newly minted models, their smiles aglow, tidy rooms of modern furniture, pictures of food that seemed to leap from the page. How sad. How cockeyed the world was. It wasn't like that here behind the drawn shades. He doubted the pictures were true of any world. They reflected fantasy too.

"All right," she said from the doorway. She attempted to smile and froze. She let the smile go and was herself again.

He took her arm lightly. She stumbled on the rug, and he caught her by the waist but let her go again when she looked afraid.

Crowds jostled them on the sidewalk. She pushed one man into the gutter. Purely reflex action. She knew how to live in the city.

The hospital was five blocks distant. He knew better than she. He had counted the blocks each day for seven days of Jimmy's confinement. He had spent his time in one place or the other, in the hospital or in her disheveled world. In between the two he counted the blocks, the cracks in the sidewalk, the passing cars, clouds, anything but the minutes wasted in limbo.

"It could have happened in the Mississippi Delta or the Alabama hill country," he said, forgetfully speaking his thoughts aloud. A mistake.

"Don't you say that." She was a hiss against his eardrums. "Don't you ever say that again when you know it's a lie."

Was it a lie? Was crime less cruel, accidents less real, disease less rampant, death less certain in the South? He wanted to believe.

She stopped and looked up at the hard marble structure blotting the afternoon sky. The floors rose out of squalor, noise, the stink of exhaust and decay. The hospital filled a space between the spires of a Catholic church on one side and a glass skyscraper on the other. He pressed her elbow and she lurched forward. He looked down at her shoes and saw they were the red, dainty ones, but they were scuffed and dirtied. One of her stockings had a run in it that followed a faint blue vein down the back of her leg, ending an inch short of the heel. He wanted desperately to hold her. But she was leaving him, and he'd lose sight of her if he didn't hurry.

Frosty air buffeted them as the doors slipped open. Too white, too scalding white and antiseptic. Employees in pastel colors moved in streams across the lobby. There was a bouquet. Clorets, Dentyne, alcohol, strong soap, pine oil. A bored receptionist, a volunteer in pink uniform and grey curls, looked up and slowly thumbed through her card file. She extracted two candy pink visitor's cards from the pile at her side and attached metal clips that hung like silver fingers from the corners. A brief, totally insincere smile. He ignored it and moved her to the bank of elevators. He knew you didn't have to talk here if you didn't want to. Social courtesies weren't enforced.

"How can you stand this?" she asked when they were safely entombed in the buzzing elevator.

"For Jimmy."

"I couldn't. Not even for you."

The doors slid apart and she looked into the glaring lighted hallway. He followed behind, gaze on the stocking run, sure the blue vein was even more prominent than it had been before.

"Are you Jimmy's parents?" a nurse called from behind a closed glass window in a cubicle. Sweat poured from her brow. She might be filling sacks with peaches on a roadside stand. "Would you wait here for a minute? The doctor wishes to speak to you."

They watched as the nurse dialed a number on the desk phone. When she finished they stared at her expectantly. She wiped her forehead and scattered a pile of pastel papers on the floor at her feet.

A voice took them from the back. "Well, hello! I'm glad you both could come. Will you follow me, please?"

Brisk, self-important footsteps. A consulting room, small, splashed with vinyl chairs in orange, yellow, green.

They faced the doctor. "Two days ago it wasn't good," he intoned. "The chances for Jimmy were slim. But I have good news. We believe he's going to pull through. The cut didn't reach the lungs. He's in stable condition, finally."

Her rigid body toppled like a tower into her husband's arms. He supported her with an arm around her shoulder. He heard her crying softly. The doctor patted her arm and left the room.

"I want to see him," she said.

Against the crisp white sheets he lay sleeping. His face was unmarked, his dark lashes calm against his plump cheeks. She touched the mound of bandages around his middle. Her fingers darted up to his chest, his chin, his lips. She pulled away and moved to the door.

Outside the hospital, he whispered close to her head as she pressed her body against his. Horns bellowed, cars belched past, sodium lights winked on to signal nightfall.

He had made up his mind. Jimmy's reprieve demanded promises.

"We'll leave as soon as he's able. We'll take a train. I'll send some applications to the park services and try to find a house, a house with a porch and a swing. We'll leave here."

"You'll take me home?"

"Yes. All three of us will go home."

At the street a cabbie slammed his brakes and squealed to a halt, narrowly missing the couple crossing the street against the light. He shook his fist and yelled obscenities until they were lost in a crowd on the sidewalk.

She remarked on the heat, the city's terrible heat, as they beat forward against the onslaught of night people seeking an avenue of escape. He stayed quiet and listened because they were inside the circle again and his comments weren't needed. He let her plot their future into Southern woodlands, her voice dipping below the city roar to reach him. He made an effort to enter the fantasy. He pushed away all doubts, all fears of what it was like where she wanted to go. If she didn't remember hate or prejudice or boredom maybe it didn't exist. He hoped she was right. She might have been right all along.

"We'll look for wild strawberries in the spring and let Jimmy taste them before he's too old," she said.

He nodded on cue. Jimmy was not yet a man. The entire country was not yet grotesque and dangerous. His wife was not yet irreversibly lost in the corridors of her own alienation. There was hope and peace and happiness. Until he found where it hid, it was his duty to protect his family, without fail, the way a giant oak supports and protects the lichens growing in feeble masses about its exposed roots.

"Don't you think so?" She asked and her voice was taking wings.

He didn't know what she was referring to, but he knew the answer. "Yes," he said quickly. "Yes, I agree."

"I know that I'm right," she said, taking his hand and rubbing his knuckles with her thumb the way she did when she was happy.

In the stale, airless apartment she raised the shades, emptied the ashtrays, sorted the magazines. He reclined on the bed watching. It was her world and he was content to let her guide him through it. She knew the landmarks so well.

MARSHA CARTER

NOTHING BUT THE BLOOD

"NOTHING BUT THE BLOOD OF Jesus," the old song enclosed her memory like a revival tent arching over the bobbing heads of hand-clapping worshipers.

"We believe," a tall, black-suited tent proselyte licked his syllables and spit them out like bad candy.

"We believe," the group chimed, desperate bells in the steamy air.

"God is he-yeh," he drawled, rolling his eyes.

"God *is* here," a woman screamed before the crowd could repeat it.

"God is *here*," the minister slapped his large hands against either side of the fainting woman's head and held her in an embrace of passion that tickled the groins of those watching.

She remembered being uncomfortably moved, sliding back between her aunt whose hips were jiggling in rhythm, and her uncle who moaned and keened blank-eyed. Between them, she was an unnoticed child. She too believed that night. She too was released from the moist heat of the tent, saved, into the clear summer night.

Her memory moved on to a morning of berry picking, to a day as simple as a green hill carving a soft breast out of a blue sky. She remembered feeling buoyant, scrambling through the stickers to grab the blackberry. Untangling her hair from the bushes, she stood up and dropped the berry into her burlap bag.

"God protects all people," her cousin Rauth had said, patting his own full sack. Its bottom was blue-stained and dripping.

"We don't never have to worry 'bout nuthin'," she replied. They stood on the side of a hill dotted with bramble bushes hiding blackberries, skinny legged and smug.

Her memory time-lapsed like a French photographer playing Renoir. Sensitive Impressionism fogged the edges of chronological events and drew her behind them, like the heroine trying not to stain the hem of her dress as she follows the camera dollie.

To believe is to be protected. To be protected is to live in grace. To live in grace is to be protected. Therefore, just believe. Rauth lasted thirty-seven days in Vietnam. His body, the face redone, was preceded by a telegram and two marines who seemed resigned to the ritual. She dreamed two dreams after the telegram came.

In the first dream she was standing on a densely green hill. The air was wet with the scent of bodies. Below her a river ran red. The red river flowed as crisp as the bright stream of blood that trickles from a superficial cut. In its waves, young men floundered. Rauth tumbled by and reached out an arm to her.

"Save me, save me," he called, "I believed."

She woke up, shaking the room into control. Falling asleep again, she dreamed Rauth stood before her. He had no face. Instead, clumps of flesh adhered loosely to his facial bones like a child's first clay sculpture, pieces stuck randomly to the wire underneath. She recognized him by his hands, which were perfectly intact.

"Would you want to live?" she asked him.

"Not with my face like this," he said.

"Nothing but the blood of Jesus," she giggled, and woke up horrified.

Her vital connection between the good life and the belief that belief would hand it to her was only slightly shaken after Rauth's mutilated body did not rise from the casket. Death after all, had violated his spirit. Her's was still intact.

*

That Renoir photographer, knowing art is irony, cameras through a bizarre garden where someone has perversely planted skinny, tight-budded roses whose thorns lift like leaves inviting a touch. She still follows behind, heroically innocent, leaping the darts, believing she cannot get stuck. Unhooking her dress hem from the thorns, she believes God has granted special protection to her ankles.

*

Her mourning for Diane was as dark and as flat as the negative she kept in an envelope in her purse. In it, she and Diane were fuzzy-featured, dark figures posing on their stomachs on a white rug, chins cupped in palms, grinning blacked-out all-American smiles.

"Pretty girls," a stranger had said, glancing at the photograph made from the negative.

Diane's funeral was in September.

"It's a Catholic church," Bede whispered. "Why are all your friends Catholic?"

"I'm into rituals," she hissed. "They comfort the living and placate the dead. There are," she paused, "no Catholic ghosts, if you've noticed."

"You're sick," Bede muttered.

"No," she sighed, "I'm not."

Crossing herself hesitantly, kneeling slightly and bouncing up, she entered the church behind Diane's six sisters. They were a double trinity, this group of siblings. Two rows of three, all redheads, dressed in shades of black, dangling alternating gold and silver crosses between small and larger breasts. They wore impeccable white gloves. She imagined those suede-embraced fingers placating the dead, gently fingering rosaries, clutching each other in a row in the front pew facing the casket, lifting an arch of white protection against the rebuilt face of their sister lying in white ruffled sleep.

Diane looked as if she were seriously considering the shape of her hands folded across her chest. Her facial expression was a mortician's masterpiece after the car accident.

They filed past the open casket, they who knew her, stunned or weeping. Death was the invisible photographer clicking their brief faces for future reference, clicking as quickly as their heels rattled across the tiled floor.

Suddenly, a woman for who Diane had once worked flipped her upper body across the casket, almost laying perpendicularly across the corpse. She began gasping rhythmically, breathing formaldehyde in careless gulps.

"What's she doing?" whispered Diane's oldest sister, to the next one.

"She's praying?" trembled the youngest one, digging the gloved nails of one hand into the gloved palm of the other.

A priest ran over to the woman, losing the formality of his collar.

"You *cannot* do this," he whispered. "You must not *do* this!"

"What is she doing?" repeated the oldest sister, staring like the Magdalene at the woman's arched backsides curving over the casket.

"She's praying?" begged the youngest one, looking around for relief or reason. Diane's oldest sister suddenly made a convulsive movement which jerked the necks of flabbergasted mourners. She pressed her fingers into her eyes, and called to all their minds without exception, the Biblical phrase, "If thine right eye offends thee, pluck it out!"

The middle sisters half rose, arms linked and rigid, staring like earthquake victims at the woman's wreaking back.

"She is praying!?" shrieked the youngest one, and pressed her fists into either side of her head, tufts of hair sprouting like thorns between her knuckles. The priest gently tugged at the woman. She did not budge, but continued breathing between the breasts of the corpse.

Small movements rippled through the seated mourners, breaking their smooth surface of civilized sorrow. Women exchanged startled glances. Men looked behind them, chins jerked to shoulder blades. Children swallowed air. In the very front, the priest was a stark rod beside the woman's heaving back. He swung around wildly, saw the crowd's face, and froze.

Lazarus must have smiled at faces like these as he stripped the death linen, stinking of oil, from his forearms. Peter, after the third cockcrow wore a face like these. Caught between panic and awe, the human face unmasks, is abandoned by spirit, and is terrible.

The scene was still life for several seconds. The tide was growing stronger, a tension which would snap, which would, which would. . . .

"What is she doing!!?" Diane's oldest sister shrieked. The room collapsed. Women slumped, men shook their heads, children howled, expelling balls of air from the chests.

Diane's oldest sister fell back into the front pew. The two staring sisters blinked like waking somnambulists. Snapped by that screaming question, the tension which tried to become a tide, which twisted muscles between shoulder blades, which pulled eyeballs, which clenched hands, and which kept them all suspended between panic and awe dropped back, licking their squirming toes.

The priest pulled the sobbing woman up, off the open casket. He stood then, hugging her to his chest, sighing with her sobs.

*

She fell on thorns. In front of her the camera dollie turns slowly, smashing skimpy roses under its wheels. The photographer too turns toward her, moving like a ballet dancer. He spins in a series of semicircles, raising his hands, palms flat and opened to her.

"This is it!" he mutters urgently. "This is it!"

Her fingertips are dripping blood. She lifts up on one elbow, holding up her fingers, staring at them as detached from her wounds as any accident victim. The photographer swings a leg over her prone and pristine martyrdom and frames her between his hands. She spits, "My fingertips are bleeding, you son-of-a-bitch!" He looks down at her and smiles. "I was wondering when you were going to say something."

She shifts out of shock into rage. "This is a tragic flaw!" She beats the ground with a splattered fist.

"It's part of the scene," the photographer shrugs.

"How," she sits up, "can my wounded hands be part of your damn scene?" He moves to her right, as casual as a snake. The camera focuses only on her. She sees herself reflected, chin narrowed, her face receding below protruding eyes.

"Because they are the result of your own decisions," his voice is compassionate. She stares. He continues. "Your decision completed the scene. I was only waiting. . . ."

"You son-of-a-bitch!"

". . . for it."

"You son-of-a-bitch!" she screeches, then swallows her scream like a knife.

He strokes the edge of a rose thorn with the toe of his boot, then says, as quiet as a diamond, "Art becomes art only when the artist releases control of it. Art is art only after it finishes itself."

"Then what is the artist?" she demands, terrified at the door of revelation.

"Someone who watches and loves." He leans forward, almost human in his need to be understood. "Believe, believe in only this."

"And all. . . ." She waves a crimson hand weakly across an invisible horizon of memory. He silently moves behind the dollie.

Slowly she turns to the camera. In its iris she is alone in a strange garden. Her choices, spread outward from the torn hem of her gown, are roses. Staining a verdant and dangerous field, they are nothing less than the blood.

LIONEL GARCIA

THE WEDDING

THE WIFE BROUGHT THE OLD man into the kitchen holding him up by the arm and steadied him as she reached for a chair. Having placed the chair behind him, she pushed him down gently, and he quivered and shook as he descended slowly into the chair. She took his hat off and threw it on the chair next to him.

"Be careful with my hat," he said in Spanish. "It cost a pretty penny."

"I don't see why he needs a hat," the wife said to me, completely ignoring him. "He never goes anywhere. Never even goes outside the house. Why the hat? I'll never know."

He remained silent, looking out the window. He was old and useless and could hardly walk.

"Get me some coffee," he said, rapping on the table with a little authority. "And some crackers," he added.

She took her time heating the coffee, and it seemed to irritate him. Finally, after much waiting and nervous anticipation on his part, she brought the coffee and a cracker and placed them before him on the table. There was an air of defiance on her part, and I couldn't help but think that it was an odd type of behavior after such a long marriage. I would have thought that, by now, she would have forgiven him for any pain that he had caused her.

The cup rattled as he picked it up from the saucer. He shook the cup as he brought it to his lips. After sucking mostly air, he said, "This coffee is too hot," and he placed the cup back with difficulty.

"He always complains," the wife said. "The coffee is too hot! The coffee is too cold!" She was standing behind a small counter that separated the kitchen from the dining table.

He ignored her and looked at me with more intensity than I had seen during the day that I had been there. His one good eye (the right one had a cataract) seemed to penetrate through me, and after a while it seemed to water excessively. Little did I know at the time that he was trying to size me up to be sure I could appreciate an event that had left a terrible impression on him.

"I must tell you what happened to me in 1900 when I was ten years old."

The wife stood up straight and went over to the sink. "He's going to tell the wedding story again. I'll bet my life he's going to do it." She looked at me and raised her hand and pointed to her temple with her index finger and made a circle in the air. "He's a little crazy from old age," she said aloud.

"The story concerns a wedding that I attended at a ranch near my childhood home. It was a typical ranch wedding. We, the children, were having a good time riding horses, throwing rocks at birds, and all the things children our age will do. But I'm ahead of the story." He took a drink from the cup, spilling a good deal. "The coffee is much better now. At least I can drink it."

He took a small piece of cracker and placed it as gently in his mouth as if he were taking communion. He followed with another sip of coffee, and then he chewed slowly, ruminating.

"In those days people were very mean," he said. It amused me that he made that statement. After all, it didn't seem to be logically connected to what we were talking about. "I don't know why they were. We don't see meanness like that very often anymore. Oh yes, one could say that our neighbor here on my right is not good, is lazy, but he is not mean."

"Don't talk about the neighbors. Don't you know any better?"

"He's always been a bad neighbor, very lazy and a scoundrel. But that's not important. I know he's lazy and a thief. Didn't he steal my rake?" he asked me. I didn't know.

"Your rake is in the garage underneath all the pile of garbage that you never cleaned in forty years of living in this house. Don't accuse the neighbors of anything. You're the one who is lazy and a scoundrel."

"The neighbor to my left is just as bad. He beats his wife until the poor woman comes running to us for help. But what can I do at my age? I'm ninety-two years old. I'll be ninety-three in eight months. If I were younger I would show him that to hit a woman is a sin against the natural order, besides it's against the law."

His wife was now sitting in a wooden chair across the counter. She was rolling her sleeves. "You certainly did a lot of hitting when you were younger, and I have the scars to prove it."

He looked past the woman as if she were not there. "To hit a woman as he hits her is against all the laws of man. But what can you do? They say she goes out on him, and at night, I seem to see a car go slowly by. I may be wrong. But I do notice that the car slows down in front of the house, and it always passes by when the husband is not around. What do you make of that?"

"He hit me many time when he came home drunk," she said to me. "But what could I do? I had children to think of. If it hadn't been for them, I would have left him years and years ago. Now the children are grown, don't like him, and don't come to visit him. I'm here stuck with him not able to see my children. I'm not sure they appreciate what I did for them. It was hard, very hard. And then he would take after the children and almost kill them with blows. He would be so drunk that he wouldn't remember, but I'll tell you this, the children never forgot, and they never forgave. Right now he could die, right where he sits, and they wouldn't care. This is the legacy that he has left behind. What is cruel for me is that, in his old age, he had no remorse. How can he? He doesn't know what day it is."

I had the feeling that I was being brought into the conversation, and I didn't want to become involved. The woman wanted desperately for me to agree with her. The old man was ignoring her.

He continued.

"One night she came in running and had blood all over her clothes. The other neighbor, of course, could care less. When I asked him about it, he said it wasn't any of his business, that he was having trouble with his wife also. To think that this is where we wound up living, among these savages. But they aren't as mean as the brothers I was going to tell you about. Do you want some more coffee?"

I replied that I had enough.

"If you need some more, just ask," he said. "Just as if you were in your own home.

"They were three brothers, mean as wolves, and they delighted in creating trouble wherever they went. Never was a person at peace when they were around. Let me tell you that they one time killed a young calf in front of his owner and asked him if he was going to fight about it. The poor man said no. Who would fight someone like that and especially when there were three?" He pointed three raised fingers at me.

"The week before the wedding they had had an altercation with the bride's father. Nothing serious by anyone's standards. The old man happened to be drinking beer at a tavern, and he said something about another man, an acquaintance of his, an innocent remark in any case, except that the brothers were there, and they took exception to the man's remark. They claimed the man being talked about was their uncle. Can you imagine that? They probably didn't even know the man. The man apologized and left, or tried to leave, I should say. They accosted him, tore off his shirt, and slapped him around. The man begged to be left alone, and they released him, warning him to be careful how he spoke from now on."

He cocked his eye at me again and held it open until a tear rolled down his face. He wiped the tear with a crooked brown finger as he continued to study me. He took another piece of the cracker and placed it on his tongue. He chewed for a while and then swallowed the cracker with some coffee.

"In any case, there was bad blood between the two parties. The man's sons, upon learning what had happened, were angry and had to be restrained from going after the three brothers.

"I remember as if it were yesterday that the wedding was on a hot August Sunday. We were in the middle of the dog days of summer, the so-called *canicula,* when even the wind will burn your face—the type of weather we had when we blazed the road from San Diego to Freer. It was so hot then that the snakes would hide under the hollow roots of the older trees. All we had to do was go to the old tree and throw gasoline at the trunk and the snakes would roll out in a tangled mess, some so angry they would strike at each other and would fight to the death locked around each other. We would take a shovel or a grubbing hoe or an ax and kill them. But the more we killed, the more there seemed to be. It was like the tale that has no ending."

He took a handkerchief from his shirt pocket with a very shaky hand and wiped drool from the corner of his mouth.

"The wedding was beautiful. All morning long people had arrived—on horseback, and wagons, and even one old car. Who brought the car?"

The woman was caught by surprise. She seemed to wake up to the question. "There were no cars in 1900. You've got your stories mixed up. The first car we saw was in 1913, 1914, somewhere around there." She returned to her thoughts.

She struck me as having a very poor attitude, and then again she had been with him so very long that she didn't care for him or his conversation. The most I could say about her was that at least she didn't constantly interrupt the old man while he spoke, only occasionally.

"The wedding itself was at about eleven o'clock that morning. There were bridesmaids and best men, and all one sees at weddings. After the ceremony, we ate barbecue. The father of the bride—Antonio was his name, Antonio Briones—had killed a calf, and his friends had barbecued it in earthen pits all night long. Needless to say, they had been drinking all night long. This is not good, for men to drink all that much."

"Look who's talking now," she said. She looked at me and made a motion like a man drinking a beer and pointed at him. She laughed. "They used to call him 'hollow leg' because he drank so much. How quickly this man forgets. I cannot believe this."

He completely ignored her. "Let me tell you why it is wrong for a man to drink a lot. After a while, he abandons his family— his wife, his children, everything dear to his heart."

She got up and left. "I can't take any more of this," she said. She walked out of the kitchen and through a door to the side of the stove. It hadn't occurred to me that there was a room behind the kitchen, but apparently there was one, for this was where she went.

"You understand that we children were not allowed in the wedding ceremonies. We were observers, and we were fed last. Each with his plate, we went to the woods to eat. We could hear the laughter of the celebrants as they ate and drank. We were happy also, but not for long. From the woods we could see three men riding across the corn field towards the house, trampling the corn as they came. You understand that to injure a man's crop is to insult him gravely. At that time we didn't know who they were. They were, in fact, the three brothers, the troublemakers, and we were to remember them for the rest of our lives.

"Remember that this happened some eight-two years ago, and I have difficulty remembering names. The father's name was Antonio Briones, and he had two sons, Adolfo and Octavio. Two of the men that had been drinking all night were the brothers Juan Garcia and Julian Garcia. The troublemakers, the mean brothers, were Juvencio, and. . . ." He couldn't remember.

"Eusebio and Carlos," came the voice from behind the kitchen.

"Eusebio and Carlos," the man repeated as if he had thought of the names himself. "And their last name?"

"Gonzales," she replied. "And quit bothering me. I'm in the middle of my rosary."

"Juvencio Gonzales rode to the long outside table where the wedding party was eating. His two brothers remained behind by the house. I could see him ride almost to the table, almost touching it, and the startled people looked up and saw him. Antonio Briones, the father, was up immediately upon seeing the man on horseback.

"'What do you fellows want? Why do you trample my crop?' The wind was blowing in my direction and I could hear their voices as if I were standing behind them. 'I thought that I had passed the word that I didn't want you at the wedding.'

"'That's the word we received,' Juvencio replied. 'And it sticks in our craw that anyone would insult us, my brothers and me, in this way. After all we did you no real harm.'

"'I have already forgotten that,' Antonio said. 'And as for my sons, they have also. You were not invited, and I'm asking you in an amicable way to leave.'

"By that time the men in the wedding party were standing up. The bride was being led quickly away. The women were almost carrying her to the house. The groom, Pablo Garcia, stood (I could see very plainly for I was directly behind a mesquite tree and hiding my body from everyone) and he, Pablo, walked to where the conversation was going on. Upon seeing Pablo approach their brother, Juvencio, the other two rode their horses up. It was then three against two.

"Antonio's sons, Adolfo and Octavio, had been in the house, and when they saw what was going on, they reached for their rifles and came out running.

"'There will be no violence,' Antonio shouted to his sons. 'This is a day for celebration and joy. Let us not destroy it!'

"I can still hear the man say those words right now as if I were still hiding behind the tree. The other children that I was with had scattered, and I could see them hiding much the same as I.

"From here on, my mind becomes very vague, as if I had seen this in a dream. The reality did not strike me until I was a young man.

"I had been looking around at my friends, when suddenly I heard a shot. By the time I looked up, (and it was almost instantaneously) all I could see was a puff of smoke rising from the barrel of a pistol held by one of the terrible brothers. My first instinct was to look at the group—who had fallen? No one! The I realized he had shot into the air. Juvencio, the oldest of the mean ones, dismounted. He had a smallish bay horse— smallish but fine looking. He pushed the father backwards, and I could see the old man trying to push back. Again he was pushed back, and I could see the men coming closer.

"'Let them fight!' shouted Eusebio, the younger of the *malos*. He knew it was not a fair fight. 'Leave them alone, and I mean it,' he said. He had a menacing look to him as he spoke to the man. 'Anyone interferes, and he has me to deal with!

"Mean Juvencio struck the father on the head and the poor man fell to his knees. Blood started flowing from the top of his head. He had been hit with some sort of instrument. Immediately I saw that it was a long barreled pistol, the same type that the Rangers used in the old days. God help you if you are ever hit on the head with a pistol such as that one. The barrel was thicker than my thumb."

He showed his thumb, a worn out wrinkled digit brown with age.

"The sons seeing their father bleeding, could not restrain themselves. Who would? Your father is bleeding profusely and on the ground, his enemy standing over him ready to shoot. They opened fire. The confusion was great as you can imagine. Juvencio fell dead but not before firing several shots into poor Antonio, the father of the bride. He also died immediately from what I could see. Now everything becomes a blur to me for the action was so fierce, so intense, that I could not follow it. There were too many things going on at one time. The women were crying and screaming in the house. They could see exactly what was going on, but they were powerless. But it seemed to me that Pablo Garcia, the groom, was the next to fall. There was no cause to kill him. But he fell by his father-in-law's side. The two surviving mean brothers, Eusebio and Carlos, were shooting at everyone, and Adolfo and Octavio were shooting at them. The women had broken through the door and were running toward the scene. The brothers Juan and Julio Garcia, unarmed, did not have a chance. Both fell as they tried to intervene.

"The thing is that Adolfo and Octavio, the old man's sons, apparently were enraged when they witnessed the father being attacked. Who wouldn't? Wouldn't you have done the same?

"After it was over, and it was over quickly, although at that time it seemed an eternity, there were eight men killed. Most children never experience the violent death of one single person in their lifetime, but here I was, on that day I had seen the death of eight men. Let me tell you who they were: Antonio Briones, the father of the bride, and one of his sons, Adolfo. Octavio survived the onslaught and had a very prolonged recuperation. He was maimed for life. Pablo Garcia, dead. He was the groom. Killed defending his father-in-law's honor. That's three. The three brothers who would cause no more problems. That's six. And the brothers Juan and Julio Garcia who had been drinking all night.

"The aftermath was horrible, even more horrible than the shooting itself. The women were on the men as soon as the shooting stopped. They were screaming and crying and could not contain their grief. They were running from body to body screaming. The bride's dress which had been white and beautiful shortly before, was now spattered with blood. She tried to hold her husband's head on her lap, but she jumped up and ran toward her father, and thus she went, torn between the two men. The bride's mother, Antonio's wife, was in a rage, and she picked up a revolver that belonged to God knows who and began firing at Juvencio, her husband's killer, even though he was already dead.

"You can imagine what an episode like that does to a child my age. I have lived with that memory for most of my life."

He was silent for a while as he looked at me with that crooked eye. He took one last piece of cracker and a drink of coffee. Then he reached over and picked up his hat by the crown. He placed it straight on his head and I noticed how large his ears were.

"Are you through?" came the voice from inside the room.

"Yes," he answered.

She came out, grabbed him by the arm, and led him away. He tried to say something, but she told him to hush. "You've talked enough already."

"Wait a minute," he said, forcefully removing her hand from his arm. "I have more to say."

"No you don't," the woman replied. "You're going to bed."

"Leave me alone!" he shouted. "Can't you see that I need to say one more thing? God damn it, why must you bother me so?"

He braced himself with his hand on the counter and swayed gently back and forth. (He didn't need her after all.) "When I was a child," he said, and a tear came down his face, "my father would take us to a small lake near where I was born. And on the surface of the lake you could see the salt as it collected and floated to the shore. We would go there and pack salt, and in the winter, we would kill the ducks that had migrated from God knows where. We would take the dead birds and wash the lice off them in the salt water, skin them—skin, feathers and all and clean them to take home. My father loved the tails. He ate them raw. He would chew the tails off the ducks just like one chews the end of a loaf of bread. My brothers and I, we would laugh and feel like vomiting, but mostly we would laugh. No one knew why the lake was salty, but you could float almost anything in it. We bathed in it during the summer, but we were never allowed to go to the deep end. Someone had told my father that it was very deep. Later on, in my older years, when I was operated on in my head for a tumor, I dreamed after the operation, while in a coma, that we were cutting large slabs of salt and loading them on mule-drawn wagons, and it seemed the dream went on forever, the salt went on forever. But," he said turning toward the woman and extending his arm to her, "those were the good days when I was like new."

I could hear her scolding him in the back room as she put him to bed. "Do you need to go to the toilet?" she asked.

"No," came the meek, childish reply. "Tomorrow maybe I can tell him about the snakes," he said.

"Shut up and go to sleep," she said. "You've already talked enough for two days."

FRANCES FLETCHER

THE PERFECT GIFT

MARYLOU MEDFORD FELT AS IF the top of her head was coming off.

She had moved graciously through the long day of phone calls and congratulations. She had been warmly thankful for the lovely presents—and they *were* lovely—from Thomas and his wife, Alice, who was every bit as good as another daughter to her, and from her own Irene and Irene's Michael.

Michael had insisted on hooking up the electric carving knife that was one of their gifts and placing her hands just so on its handle.

"See, Mom," he explained carefully. "Nothing happens 'til you pull this trigger here. That's the only thing to remember. Not scared of it, are you?"

"Of course not," she had lied. All new electric gadgets were capable of scaring Marylou. She remembered with more than a trace of regret the days of kerosene lamps and wood stoves.

When the grandchildren had sung "Happy Birthday" as Irene set the glowing cake before her, Marylou's eyes had shone with warm, affectionate tears. It had all been wonderful. She was grateful. And now she was tired to death. At seventy-nine, perhaps she had a right to be.

At last, they were all going home, crowding out of the hallways of her little house. Nobody had far to drive. Both families lived in the same large suburb as Marylou did.

Birdie next door, lingering on her lawn to wave at the departees, stepped across the driveway now and said it once more. "Don't know how lucky you are, Marylou, having the kids so close to you—and having kids that take such good care of you."

Marylou smiled into Birdie's warm, round face. "Ninety percent of the time I think so, too," she said. "It's just that, once in awhile, I begin to feel a little crowded."

Birdie was really a little shocked at that. "Oh, how can you *say* that! Why, Thomas has that big, successful dental practice to look after, but he never fails to call you every day, just to check!"

"I know . . . I know . . . and Irene, even with her mornings working at the library, nearly always comes by during the afternoon to see if I need any shopping or have any errands. Such really *good* children."

"So, how come you're complaining?"

"I'm not, really. Only, you know, Birdie, I think the children had more . . . more respect for me before Lyle died. All the time we were still a couple, they looked on me as a competent member of society. Why, they used to ask my advice."

"I know what you mean." Sometimes Birdie surprised her with a sudden, endearing plunge into insight. "But look at it from their point of view. They were depending on your husband to do the looking after until he went, five years ago. Since then, you've given up driving. . . ."

"Because they wanted me to," Marylou interposed.

"And they were right! This city's gotten too big for you; everybody goes faster than you want to drive. And there's four of them to run errands for you. Besides, you can walk to the bus lines if you want to go downtown."

"Which I don't! But you're right, Birdie, I'm a lucky woman. And I'm taking my lucky self into the house for a nice hot bath and bed, right now!"

It was a blessing to have Birdie, a retired practical nurse, next door, Marylou thought as she soaked in the tub. There were plenty of other friends, too. Retired teachers like herself, to call on the phone or meet for coffee at one or another's home. Marylou enjoyed them as she did her church friends, a little at a time. Seen every day, she had to admit, most of them would be dull, dull, dull.

"Our conversations are so limited," she had once complained to Alice. "Grandchildren, recipes, these scandalous modern times, the iniquities of the government. Or worst of all, our different aches and pains."

Surely there should still be something more.

The present! She had forgotten the present! Just like an old woman, Marylou scolded herself, hastily draining the tub, drying off, hurrying down the hallway with her quilted robe flapping. It had come in the afternoon, special delivery, luckily before the children—and their children—had arrived for the party.

Seeing that it was from her favorite nephew, whom the family dubiously referred to as the Wild One, Marylou had not held out against temptation, but had opened the mysterious, heavy box right away. Fortunately!

Adam was the only one in the family who shared her obstinate love of privacy. Perhaps for that reason, in him alone she had confided her crazy dream. He had been quite a young man then, visiting her between college semesters just because he wanted to.

She had made his favorite sandwich, grilled cheese with homegrown tomato slices and bacon on top. They had feasted and had a momentous conversation.

"I don't know exactly what I want," he had said. "But it has to be motors—machines—engineering, you know. Maybe airplanes. Not flying them, but designing them. That's what I want to spend the rest of my life doing. It's all I dream about."

"I have a dream, too." Now, what had made her say that, when she had never even told Lyle about the crazy thing?

Adam looked interested and waited.

"I'd like, just once, before I die, to . . . to . . . fly."

He was surprised. "But you've flown, Aunt. Don't you remember when you came up to spend Thanksgiving with Pop and Mom? And two or three other times, haven't you?"

"Oh, yes, dear, but I don't mean in a plane. I mean, you know, by myself." How *peculiar* it sounded! Anybody but Adam would have been phoning for the men in the white coats, she supposed. "Don't you know, they have a kind of apparatus you can strap on. I saw it demonstrated on the television two or three years ago, on the news. A man had it on his back and he just floated over a bunch of parked cars."

"Oh, I know what you mean. But, Aunt!" His chuckle grew into a laugh, and in a minute Marylou was laughing with him.

"It is funny, I suppose, for a proper English teacher like me, just when I'm getting on toward my old tabby days . . . but still. . . . Oh, I could never pay for such a thing, of course. And the noise it made! Horrible! But when I saw it, and the man really, really flying, I thought, 'Maybe they'll make a model even I could use, before I get too old to try it!' Come on, now, don't you think it would be wonderful?"

Adam had been serious then, and had agreed with her. Of course it would be beautiful, just flying around by oneself. Someday, he thought, it would happen.

That conversation had been a long time ago. She hadn't consciously thought of it again until today, when she had opened the present.

It was a flying machine.

Not that she would have known by looking at the compact, elegant bronze mechanism. The letter inside the box had explained.

"I've been working on this surprise for a long time, Aunt. Knowing you, I knew you hadn't given up that old dream. We've learned a lot since you and I talked about flying so long ago.

This is a pilot model, strictly experimental, but I've personally tested it thoroughly. You wouldn't be getting it now if I wasn't sure it was safe!

"The three cylinders in the small boxes are the energy cells. That's our one remaining hang-up—finding a way to produce them in quantity. You put one of them into the compartment marked 'A' on the drawing, and snap the bottom closed. Controls are on the wide strap that goes around your waist. Study it carefully before you try anything! The instruction booklet tells you everything.

"Auntie, maybe this is a crazy present to send you. I'm not sure myself, but I'm sure Irene and Tom will think so! I feel this way about it: you've done what other people wanted you to all your life. Why shouldn't you please yourself just for once? I want to see my favorite relative have herself a ball!"

Dear Adam, she thought, stowing away the box— surprisingly light, it seemed, for such an apparatus—in her closet. Maybe I'll never use it, but I love you for thinking I might.

Next morning she was up early and waiting for the downtown bus as soon as the department stores opened. She went to a large, medium-priced store where nobody would know her.

"A jump suit?" the young clerk asked, swinging her long, untidy hair. "What size, ma'am?"

"I'll have to try something on," said Marylou. "Perhaps a ten, to start with."

"This is for *yourself*, ma'am?" Amazement made her pop her gum frantically. Little old ladies buying jump suits! Something new to tell on her coffee break.

Marylou summoned all her years of teaching high school English. She stood up very straight and gave the sleazy-looking girl one long, summarizing look from head to heel and back again.

"Naturally," she said icily.

She hadn't lost her touch. The girl pulled up out of her slouch. She seemed to have swallowed her gum. "*Yes,* ma'am!" She began digging into the clothes on the rack.

Trying it on again at home, Marylou was pleased with the fit and comfort of the suit. Of course, Adam hadn't thought of the absurd figure one would make, flying about in a summer dress!

It was four-thirty, a lovely summer afternoon. She had on the suit; she had studied the manual 'til she had it by heart; what was there to wait for? Trembling a little, she hoisted the apparatus onto her back, where it rested on its own leather shield. Leather straps came over her shoulders to meet a wide front bib. Like the belt, the bib was bronze clamped onto a leather backing. The bronze portions held a variety of clearly labeled buttons as well as the energy cell compartment.

She fastened all buckles, flexed her arms. It was secure and comfortable, and not very heavy at all. The only bulky part was the back, where twin exhaust pipes ran down the shoulder blades to curve slightly outward at her waist.

Cautiously, she stepped out into the backyard, tiptoeing in the tennis shoes she had bought to go with the jump suit. Wouldn't do to have Birdie next door spot her and run out for a chat over the fence.

Nobody. Marylou stood in the exact center of the yard. Her thumb on the "On" switch, she hesitated. Did she really want to do this? Who knew what might happen up there? Why should she take the risk? What was she proving?

"Nothing at all—except that I'm still alive!" she said fiercely to herself, and pushed the button.

There was a great jolt, as if a giant hand had tossed her upward. She gasped in a breath. She was zooming straight up into the sky. Air rushed past her face as it had when she, as little girl, used to lean out of the window of the car. There was hardly any noise. She looked down, incredibly far, to see her own back yard shrinking away.

"Don't go too high," she reminded herself from the booklet. Now, how. . . ? Ah, the "Forward" button. Next over. She pushed it. At once she was gently thrust forward, lying, it seemed, on the wind. It was the dream of her childhood.

Now she was playing with the controls. It was possible to turn, to glide, to swoop down and up and around. She grew drunk with excitement and a surging sense of power. She was young again. She was happy. She was free!

She was lost!

Where was she? There lay the great, sprawling city beneath her, but where was her own familiar suburb? She had remembered to secure her bifocals with a ribbon tied around her head, but she couldn't identify the buildings she used to know in the downtown section, even when she glided low. There were too many new ones towering above the old. Besides, she had never seen them from this angle before.

Like a providence, a police traffic control helicopter rattled into sight, above and to her right. Using her newfound skills of maneuvering, Marylou glided under it and eased herself up to the driver's window, wary of the rotor blades above.

The driver was squinting straight ahead. His partner was talking into a microphone. there wasn't a chance of being heard above the chopper's deafening noise. She would have to pantomime asking for directions. She rapped on the window with her wedding ring to get the driver's attention.

He was a big, dark fellow, she would have said, with an olive complexion; but as he turned full face to her, she saw that he turned a pasty white—almost green, in fact.

Steadying herself at the window with her left hand, Marylou courteously waved "Hi" with her right hand. Carefully she mouthed, "Where am I?"

The driver's eyes rolled up in his head. He sagged against his seat belt in a dead faint. His partner's mouth flopped as he stared across the unconscious pilot at Marylou.

"*Do* something, man!" she shouted impatiently, and then, carefully mouthing, "He's sick. Push his head down . . . HEAD . . . DOWN."

The partner seemed little better than a moron. He continued to sit frozen, staring at her. She tried once more: "WHERE . . . AM . . . I?"

Nothing. Then, like a lunatic, he jerked at the controls. She swerved away just in time to miss the huge blades as the man spun the helicopter down and away.

Marylou felt betrayed. A fine way for a policeman to act! And she still didn't know where she was. Then she thought about the sun. It was in the west, of course, and she lived in the southwest area. She must fly toward the sun until she found the great freeway system that ringed the city. Then she could glide above it to the point where it passed near her own neighborhood.

There it was! She turned left to follow it, astounded at the solid-looking miles of cars inching along the broad paved ribbon. Five o'clock traffic. She settled into "slow forward" speed at a comfortable height to read the freeway signs.

Directly below, there was a noise like two big empty boxes striking together. BONK! As she recognized it for two cars colliding and looked down, more sounds arose: BONK-Bonk-Bonk-BONK-BONK! Horrified, Marylou saw a chain of collisions below her. A whole line of cars was piled up. Most of them were just pushed into each other a little, but a small economy car in the middle was pleated like an accordion at both ends. A man was wriggling out of the window.

There were more BONKS! What in the world was happening to all those drivers? Mass hysteria, perhaps. Marylou circled confusedly, wondering how she could help them. BONK-BONK-Bonk! Every lane was tied up now, with cars behind the collision areas at a standstill as far as she could see. The man had gotten out of the window, now. He looked up and waved at her. Waved?

He was shaking his fist at her!

Oh, horrors! She turned a sharp left and hit the "Fast Forward" button. Let her get away from those cars. It was she they'd been staring at when they'd banged into each other! How awful! She was the cause of all those collisions!

There, blessedly, was the water tower for her suburb. Now she could glide quietly home and take the thing off and never, never again. . . .

Cars. Irene's and Thomas's and . . . was that the fire department's little emergency car? It was. At her house. Oh, Lord, what now?

Hoping to get in unnoticed through the back, Marylou glided down into the backyard. No chance. There stood Alice, frozen, staring up at her with her mouth open. Oh, well. Marylou touched down with her feet and remembered to cut off the motor, but the sudden shift of power unbalanced her. She sat down inelegantly in the strawberry bed.

Alice took a single step toward her and fainted dead away. Mike, Irene, and Thomas rushed out the back door. They were all talking at once; yelling, really, babbling questions, picking up Alice, lifting Marylou to her feet. Impossible to communicate with them until they calmed down.

Impossible to communicate with anybody, suddenly. A big fist seemed to close in on her chest. Infinitely surprised, Marylou gasped for breath. The pain was incredible. She flopped a weak hand at Thomas, who looked into her fact then stared harder. His voice was suddenly eight years old. "Mom!"

So this was a heart attack, she thought. I never knew it would hurt so much. She barely noticed they were lifting her, carrying her not into, but around the house to the emergency car. Somebody had taken the flying machine away. They laid her on the cot in the back. A man in a white jacket squatted beside her. Lyle, she thought, it'll be good to see you again. Wait for me.

Two weeks later she was at home again. "A mild attack—just a warning, really," Fred Cameron had assured her with his best bed-side hand-pat.

"Call that mild? You ought to try it yourself," Marylou had snapped, but she was really just playing his game. She was too thankful to get home to make any fuss.

They lined up around her bed when she was settled at home: her beloved, shocked children. Marylou noted sadly how hard they were trying to keep calm, not to disturb her. Poor things, if they weren't so afraid for me, they'd let me have it!

Michael reassured her, "There wasn't anybody really hurt in those cars on the freeway, Mom. Nobody had been moving fast enough to get hurt. Of course, there was one monumental traffic jam!"

"It was on the television every newscast for the next three days!" Alice said.

As to the damaged cars, Michael told her, most if not all of the drivers were insured. "It's still each driver's responsibility to keep his eyes on the road," he added gravely, "no matter *what* goes flying around overhead."

"Who, whom did they—did they know it was me . . . I mean, I?" She seemed to be, at least temporarily, shocked right out of her pronoun case.

Irene said most of the newscasters had decided that some trick of sunlight had created a mass optical illusion above the freeway.

A psychiatrist had explained at some length how male drivers with dark, repressed sex urges would translate this optical freak into the vision of a woman.

A small but shrill element of the population was ready to go on the witness stand to swear they'd seen a flying saucer.

Thomas told her how they'd happened to gather at her house with an emergency vehicle standing by. "Birdie next door ran over. She knew you hadn't gone out. She was bringing you some figs. When she couldn't get in the front or back, and couldn't make you hear, she called Alice. Knew you didn't nap in the daytime."

Alice added, "I panicked, I guess. Thought you must be ill—maybe fainted in here by yourself. So I called the emergency car and dashed over."

They had all congregated, and, getting no response, they had gone inside with Mike's key and were just searching the place when she had returned.

"I must have slipped the catch on the back door when I stepped out," Marylou murmured.

Irene, who was going to stay with her for a few days, smoothed her pillow.

"Are you comfortable, Mother? Good. Now, we want you to make us a promise."

"I know, dear."

Thomas burst out, "Adam must have been out of his mid, sending you that thing! Damn fool. . . !"

"Now, Thomas, I won't listen to any more of that! Adam remembered that it was a silly old dream of mine, being able to fly like that. Just once, he wanted to make a dream come true for somebody he loved."

Michael said, "But, Mother, he should have remembered. . . ."

"He only forgot one thing, Mike; he forgot that I am old and decrepit."

There was a startled silence. Quickly she added, "Of course, you all are perfectly right. It was a crazy thing for an old woman like me to do. And I want your minds to be completely at rest. I'm going to put that machine away—among my souvenirs. All those collisions! I never was so horrified in my life! I promise you, I won't endanger people like that again, not for anything!"

Irene picked up the small hand that Marylou was resting on that side of the bed and held it against her cheek. "Thank you, Mother."

A month later, when she had the house to herself once more, Marylou faithfully carried the machine to the closet in the spare bedroom. She had promised to put the machine away among her souvenirs, and she had promised never again to endanger lives as she had, flying above the freeway in daylight like that.

What about at night? Just, say, the one night . . . she had her old black opera cape somewhere, and a conical hat wouldn't be hard to make from cardboard . . .tied on with black ribbons, perhaps . . . a thrill for the children!

Smiling, she fastened down the lid and slid the storage box back into place. Neat lettering on the top said, "Halloween."

ENID JIMENEZ

LOCKED IN / LOOKED OUT

I'VE NEVER BEEN WHERE THEY thought I was. No, even now I've made plans—other plans that don't include darkness. And I've never wondered what anyone else was up to, not even youth. Everything will destroy itself in a couple of decades or so . . . it doesn't matter who helps the destruction along. I prefer to wait for the outcome. And I would never say "I told you so." That wouldn't be truthful. I don't lie out loud. I've never been lonely, either, but I would like a game of chess now and again. Solitaire is a game that I always win. I beat myself, I imagine, and although winning is frightening, to some people, I'm not afraid of losing either.

You can tell a murderer right off. It's not a special gleam in the eye like everyone says . . . it's the hands. They act separately from the body. They say, "it's time," when the mind says, "it's time." You stand still, and your hands become the assassins. The assassins; the sins. And yet, I can see, in my mind . . . a jungle without boundaries and limitless green. Then I awaken.

If I were to say that I'm not afraid, that would be lying, and I've told you already that lying is the only thing I don't do . . . well. I'm not ashamed either to tell you that I'm just like you, let's talk. I've talked to lawyers, judges, desks, and benches. I'm locked in. As locked in as one gets without being on an island, surrounded by waves and scorching sun—Africa. There are some deserted islands left, it's a constant. I had seen canaries, and zoos, and all those things you think of when you think of "locked up"; it's not like that, either. For one thing, you begin to talk to yourself; on the second day you answer.

I've always been good at stories. In here, I've gotten very good. I can break your heart. Love stories. Hate stories. War stories. Then I get too pure. I distill war until it is just two men in the desert, biting each other, kicking, screaming, locked together in eternity. Eternity makes some people quite somber. Not me. I know that you can't erase the original war; we still wear our bones on the inside to prove that.

Do you see; it's because of this, that everything is so easily explained in terms of post office lines and bridges and teacups and immunizations? And that's why some of us are locked in. Something else . . . if anyone assumes that physical containment precludes travel, then they have never allowed their mind to use its legs.

An imagination can slice the ocean up into edible pieces or walk onto an old western movie set by swinging open bar doors and spilling light on expectant bad guy faces. An imagination can dangle upside down in an animal snare and bite its leg off to escape. I've done these things and more. I know they think I'm here, but I have gone on to bigger, much better places.

I could tell you how I got here. I could tell you that I haven't the dark soul I thought was a prerequisite to murder. I've always gone at least far enough out of my way to buy Girl Scout cookies, and sometimes I would remove my hat in movie houses. I had no trouble murdering her, though, because she asked for it.

She took me to her house, after all, and pulled pieces of herself from high school annuals and memory boxes . . . dust filled the room as she hollowed herself out; preparing. We got good and goddamn drunk, too . . . cheap stuff . . . good and goddamn drunk. A murderer doesn't have a dark soul like I thought, just an understanding of endings.

It might have all began in childhood; what doesn't? I guess some of us here are born older than others. Most of what I did back then was in the name of science. My only friend as I was growing up was a scarecrow of a kid named Roger. His hair was the color of violin rosin, and freckles dotted his face in three separate constellations. We were accused of murder more than a few times. The judgment of the neighborhood weighed more heavily on our respective families, however, who were consistent in their punishment—Roger and I were separated on a weekly basis. One summer, we froze thirty-six frogs in my mother's deep freeze—right next to the vanilla almond ice cream and six frozen-eyed flounder. My mother lost ten pounds that summer because she couldn't bear to reach in behind the icy toads to get the ice cream. Eventually, when she could bring herself to endure the reach, she discovered she didn't want the ice cream anyway. Roger and I considered this an important discovery . . . much more important than the simulated "end of hibernation," when we thawed the poor things out on what must have been the hottest day of July. They moved slowly at first, dripping and steaming just a little. We ate watermelon and spit out the seeds as the frogs must have endured the greatest of all reptilian shocks—the immediate scalding of what had previously been nearly frozen blood. Thirty-six toads gave their lives for science that afternoon and two pink-stained, sticky children carried the burden of thirty-six tiny souls to bed with them that night. That was my first nightmare, by the way—it was much like a Japanese film I had just seen a few weeks before the toad massacre. I called out for my mother in my sleep just as the giant steaming toad ate my body, save the left leg which he left dangling from the carport rooftop like a Christmas tree decoration. I don't know what nightmares Roger had that night, but they must have been bad. He started attending mass even more often than before (it might have been a coincidence because his sister began wearing dresses that same summer), and he and I drifted apart. I bring all this up because, as I've mentioned, he was my only real friend and the last person who could hold a conversation with me without first packing it full of recommendations.

I had once gone to church with him to see what he found so attractive about it all. The stained glass held my attention for awhile, with all of the pictures of slaughtered animals and woeful sinners and children who peered between purple-lined clouds to see God or a golden cup. One pane was of Jesus, who was talking to the masses with extended hands; the next pane over was Jesus on a cross with nails in his palms. Religion seemed very cause and effect if you looked at it only through the stained glass illustrations. Eating wafers and drinking wine sounded a lot better than it turned out to be. For one thing, we all had to use the same cup and you didn't even get enough wine to make you a little drunk. Roger must have enjoyed that kind of stuff, though, because he became very serious about it all. I'd like to think he got into it for the girls; after all, that's how I got where I am today. He might have fallen for some girl or another without realizing that Catholic girls cross their legs as well—especially those who "intend" to become nuns. He can't tell me he wasn't interested at one time, either; I knew him then. I really knew him.

I didn't have any enemies then; everyone was too frightened of me to hate me out loud. Kids tried to avoid me without catching them avoiding me. I wasn't a bully; I was a scientist. I had a conscience, though, and Roger was a firm believer in that. If I didn't like someone, they were fair game for my experiments. My grandmother proclaimed to everyone that I was just mature for my age, which made some of the things I did more palatable for the family pride in general. It wasn't only the "animal experiments" that made me out of the ordinary—it was my uncanny disconcern for what people thought about what guilt was, and although Roger tried to explain it to me, my reputation already was terribly tarnished.

I didn't surprise my family in the least when I ended up here. They all knew I would end up here. What they didn't know is that I haven't ended up—I've just begun a new experiment. I travel. That may be strange to hear from someone who lives in a 12x12 cubicle; from someone who has a constant shadow of black bar slashes on his face. I admit I worried a little, at first. The day they brought me in, for example, I paced. I remember quite plainly, that I ran to the bars to ask the guard for a transfer to a larger room. I told him that I would go crazy in such a small place, and that I wanted a room facing the courtyard instead of the injecting chamber walls. There was a possibility for a less gruesome place, I thought. He said something that I still believe to be profound, no matter the source. He said, "You're all crazy in here. Look what side of the bars you're on. If you were sane, you'd be out here." Then he walked away, as if it were a natural thing to walk away from a man who had just been condemned to trudge through the mire of his own memories or to invest a whole new personage into a whole new world he would have to invent inside a 12x12 block room that faced his inevitable doom. Roger told me once that heaven was described in the Bible as being just about this small; but he was given to exaggeration if he felt it helped get the point across.

He came to see me a while back. He's a Father now. Father Roger. He asked me some questions, of course, to make sure that my mortal body had committed the actual act and not my immortal soul. Father Roger tended to believe my theory about the hands acting separately from the soul. In a way, I feel sorry for Father Roger; his best friend grew up to be a murderer. He promised to return tomorrow morning though. Everyone was surprised that I would allow the last rites to be given, since I'm not a Catholic. I did it for Roger. Why not? Personally, I think murderers don't give a damn about what people think they deserve. The just take anything that's offered.

Like her, for example. The cafe door opened. I looked up, automatically, not really caring to see anyone in particular. When she walked in, red dust from the road shook off her. She threw her head back; dust like glitter in the sunlight that had been allowed in the open door swirled into my coffee. She walked over to my booth and sat down. Just like that. No "may I" or "my name is" . . . just sat. For that moment, I thought of a jungle somewhere. A jungle absorbing the day, trailing mosquitoes and the scent of flowers behind it. I thought of this because she made me feel . . . as if she was a movement of the leaves; like a deer . . . and I was supposed to crouch for the attack.

Yes, it was strange. I tell you it was like life had stopped following her around weeks before. Just the sight of her made my blood being to race. She spoke—the empty sound of wind. Within the hour, I knew her life as well as my own. Anyone who can relate a life story so well, considers it over with already. Before too long, she began to expect sympathy, first, then we had some pound cake. It must have been a week old because I remember her remark about how it tasted like a sweater. That's the only thing I remember her saying, and we talked all afternoon.

She was a stranger after all; not an enemy, or a friend. I began to wonder if an experiment was presenting itself to me. Sure. I had to be careful . . . the previous experiment had lost me my job; the one prior to that, well, my family doesn't want to talk to me anymore. Perhaps that worked out for the best because they can work on each other so much more efficiently without me causing so much scandal. I use the word scandal loosely here; it was a shame but all of their plans to denounce me were worthless when the media interviewed them on my capital punishment case. Each and every one of them had his opportunity to tell everyone how much I deserve everything I get. Anyway, I knew that caution was at a premium when you experiment with adults, but I rationalized that what else was destiny but a string of experiments? My failures could have been considered catastrophes by someone less objective. I had nothing of value left, and I didn't even know what "value" meant. Who could have projected that a quiet diner, like any other you see on the side of the highway . . . and a cup of coffee would begin a new adventure? Just coffee, I thought in my innocence as I stopped my journey, then I'll finish hitching to Dallas. I had hopes that a purpose would present itself to me in Dallas. I found something interesting on the side of highway 380 instead. The rest of the story is just details. They aren't as important as what I learned. I learned that I have the capacity to feel so sorry for someone that I will do anything for them. At least I did it that once. I thought that a strange discovery about myself, and I felt almost human about it. I know that murder isn't really a starting point in the quest for being a great humanitarian, but I was concerned enough about someone else to carry out a request—at the expense of my freedom. She asked me to go home with her; she had been desperate for someone—anyone. I was anyone enough for her.

It wasn't that she wasn't beautiful, either. People have been murdered for that before, you know. Imagine waking up one morning and finding an ugly old woman where your wife once lay. She was beautiful, though, especially afterwards.

That, I imagine, was the last "real" thing that happened to me. By "real," I mean that after that, my physical freedom was clipped and trimmed and finally honed into these four walls. I'm locked in, all right. But, as you can see, I've only really traveled since the day I came here. Father Roger tried to save me, he said. He asked me about my faith, wanting to know if it had diminished any since he knew me. The truth was that it hadn't, because I'd never had it back then, either. I told him that I liked parables, though. I even have one of my own.

It's a recurring dream that I call "blood sea island." I'm not an active participant in this dream, but I've attached meaning to it. The dream always begins the same: Thousands of bronzed people line the shores of what appears to be a small white-sanded island. This island is of the variety with beautiful flowers and where every kind of fruit is represented. An inactive volcano points ineffectually toward a clear, blue sky, and I know there are toucans in the leaves of the banana trees. The odd thing is the stance of all the islanders—they are all uniformly, as well as distortedly, peering out over the ocean toward the horizon in an eerie, unflinching manner. It's as if one single eye is formed from their union; an eye that creaks from left to right in a predetermined pattern they all know by heart. They don't see what they seek, and are very unhappy. Suddenly, after what I perceive is the passage of a great amount of time, they see a speck in the distance. The waves force the speck closer until it becomes a raft; closer still, it is a raft with the figure of a man on it. It's at this point that I realize that these islanders are afraid of the water. I know then, by a sudden burst of historical insight, that several of the islanders have tried to escape before by swimming. As one of them touched the water, froth and bubbles became scarlet as the body was pulled down by an unknown force, and bones were returned surprisingly clean. I became one of the silent crowd, then, warning this gentleman not to leave his raft lest he be consumed as well. The man does, though, much to our discomfort. As we crane our singular neck, his quick strokes bring him in the one hundred yards or so to the island, leaving his raft bobbing forlornly in the unending expanse of blue ocean. He doesn't say anything to us, but at once we assume he is our savior. He points at us individually, explaining without words that we are to swim one by one to the raft and be taken away from this paradise. I become increasingly uncomfortable as I watch the islanders' faces. Each one registers unwillingness to remain on the island even one moment longer now that a means of escape is at hand. The danger is very evident to me—cooperation is the only way in which this task can be completed. On my invisible yet concrete-laden lips are the unheard words of a cliché: "women and children first." They jump into the water in a single body; the ocean immediately beginning to become animated by their arms and legs and faces—scratching, reaching, flailing, clutching, and finally bleeding, frothing, and drowning.

"Cause and effect," I told Roger, "is the only way to perceive religion." I'm sure he has forgiven that insight, however, as he's consented to perform the ceremony after all.

As I told you before, I've become very good at stories in here. "Blood sea island" is just a dream. Stories are my dreams made into memories. Those are the kind I collect. I've been too caught up in mind-traveling to worry about real destinations, schedules, time, and geography—all moot points. The war stories I mentioned earlier are the most emotional journeys for me. I must really prepare myself for anything when I depart for a war. The problem I've come up against is that, like I was saying, I distill war into its purest form. I pit two men against each other, causing me to assume the unhappy roles of the thousands of widows and children, as well as the millions of grieving friends left behind to set the world in order after it's all said and done. Sometimes I forget why I even started the war in the first place, but I cover well. I like the victory parades best of all. When the clowns with the confetti pepper the car of the winning side, and the loser is forced to walk behind with a broom These war stories are usually the closest I can come to observing morality—of course, *I* get to choose the winning side. Usually the side that shows initiative has nothing to worry about. In other words, the side that is fighting to experiment with possible outcomes—that's the winning side. I admit a possible bias there, but tell me, does God feel differently?

Now I feel compelled to negate any suspicions as to my considering myself a God; I'm merely a mild megalomaniac. Forgive me, but when you re-create your own universe within a very limited physical territory—well, I call it an accomplishment. Think of the Old West, or any unconquered wilderness for that matter. That's wide open territory. Think now about generations of people feeling good about "owning" that land, presiding over it, being "gods" of its destiny. And I have done so much more with so much less.

Death row doesn't have to be a dramatic place, especially for a scientist. A person's last night of life doesn't have to be more memorable than any other—the next day will erase the memory so quickly that it might not have ever happened. I have been studying my hands, though. Tomorrow they won't be part of me anymore. My hands, the assassins, will go along their way toward dust.

I have imagined an execution—to prepare myself. Not an injection, of course—I chose instead to see a hanging. In the afternoon; a man fell from a ladder to the full extension of a rope and dangled like a ripe plum; I couldn't have been more graphic. When the sun began to set, I watched the outline of his form on the horizon—such a beautiful sunset; so many colors. To further calm myself, I gathered clouds that kneeled on the sun to push it to the other side of the world.

I might as well tell you that tomorrow I won't be there when I receive the injection; I'll be reliving "blood sea island." The man in the boat will swim toward the island. The sun will be unbearably hot, and the toucans will be screeching at each other in the woods behind us. This final time he'll have a face . . . a kind one. He'll explain to the islanders that they must come one by one onto the raft if they are to survive at all. They will jump into the water and the frenzy will begin. I will stand on the white, stark-white sand and watch, glancing now and again at the volcano and the sky. All of the islanders will die, and their bones will float away with the tide. Then there will only be the young man and myself. We will swim to the raft. We'll climb aboard and wait until the sun dips itself like a communion waver into the sea. Then we'll chart our course by the stars. I might even cast a line to catch an ugly drumhead, which will thump himself on the floor of the raft in a final frantic code of uselessness. Then, when the injection works, perhaps I'll be able to travel even further than before. My plans don't include darkness; I've told you before.

The sunlight is filtering into my small window to be strained into black slashes on the floor. I awakened to curt footsteps not ten minutes ago, yet, they only peered in to check on me. I have begun to prepare for my journey. My arms relax; my mind begins to walk around the room, then into the courtyard, then I am suddenly thrust into the glaring sunlight of the island. A man, meanwhile, has entered my cell with a tray of food. I have never explored the island before, so I decide to take a walk. The jungle is greener from the inside and the leaves slash my face with light, like my window back there . . . where another man in a green smock comes in apologetically to remove the tray. I run through the woods now . . . faster than I have ever run before . . . I am an animal. In the leaves I hear a rustle and turn to see a deer, or a woman, I'm not sure . . . the guard who had advised me about sanity came and cuffed my body to him . . . but I am in the jungle . . . running, breathing between the leaves of a tree. Behind me, a toucan—AAAHH! I sense everything so much more keenly. I guess because I'm suddenly vulnerable; perhaps I'm more powerful in that vulnerability. I am led into the injection room where a bright overhead light swings back and forth in a mad attempt to imitate the sun, but it is here with me . . . and the deer running just ahead of me. The deer with legs shorter than mine; she had told me that she had seen things before . . . so painful that she could not stand . . . life anymore . . . "I see only limitations before me . . . so many hurdles to jump" . . . I jump; I devour . . . I have dragged so many carcasses home in one lifetime; it must be me. I remember it all too plainly for it to have been someone else; there is someone else . . . Father Roger, is that you? I'm sorry you came after all, I didn't come to greet you . . . because I'm looking in the distance on the shore now. The islanders and I are searching for that man on the raft . . . I see the needle enter my arm. . . . He is swimming for the shoreline . . . I'm still hopeful . . . the bodies pile onto one another as if freedom were that easy. Father Roger is saying something I can't make out . . . the hot lamp is still swinging . . . or is it the sun? Yes, the sun is swinging . . . I am swimming to the raft in long, easy strokes . . . the sun goes out for good.

CHRISTOPHER DOW

MEETINGS WITH ARTHUR

PLAYING TAG AROUND THE SCHOOL yard was a real obsession for me in third grade. My sister, Amy, was four years older than me and scorned such childish games. Since she went to the big school next door to the one I went to, and I thought she was wise in the ways of the world, I was a bit hurt by her offhand attitude toward my favorite pastime. Though I often tried to get back at her by making fun of her stuffed animal collection or her friends, I never really seemed to get much satisfaction. But despite her disparagement, I couldn't help but talk about the game to her as we rode home on our bicycles each afternoon.

The way home lay over a hill and down a valley, two or so miles. By injunction of our parents, we always rode together. I guess they must have felt we were safer that way. Or at least that I was safer. The arrangement was fine except when one of us had to stay after school. Then the other had to wait, too. As I was primarily the one kept late for minor infractions, Amy was justifiably grumpy on such occasions. On the day the business with the train started, we were running late for just such a reason, though not terribly so. Just the same, Amy was as angry as if I'd had to stay later. The reason was that if we didn't beat the 3:45 freight, we'd have to spend several minutes waiting for the train to pass. Naturally, this would put us home even later than ever, and Amy would miss most of her favorite afternoon TV program.

"Come on, you dodo," she said to me. "Hurry, or we'll get caught by the train."

We were pushing our bikes up the long hill from the school. That was the hardest part of the trip. Once we reached the top, we could coast down the other side, cross the railroad tracks at the bottom, then ride down the road that paralleled the tracks until we reached our home street. The way wasn't difficult, and the only thing that could go wrong would be a train blocking us.

We reached the top of the hill, and as we mounted our bikes, we looked to see if the train was coming. Though the road that led to the bottom was winding for most of its length, and the bottom was hidden from a viewer at the top, there was a portion of track that could be seen through a break in the trees and houses covering the slope of the hill. This section of track was down to the left of where we stood, and about three-quarters of a mile away. The train would pass across this section of track before it reached the crossing at the bottom of the hill, and if we could see it through this perspective window, then we could be certain we'd have to wait for it to pass when we got to the bottom.

No train was visible, and Amy shouted to me to come on. Then she started down the hill, pedaling at first, then braking as her momentum built up. I followed as fast as I could, but I was still a novice bike rider, cautious of the steepness of the hill and the many turns. Amy was soon out of sight, though I tried to keep up with her.

About half way down the hill was another perspective window, showing another section of track, a bit closer to the road crossing. As I looked through this, I saw the train passing by. I slowed down, not so much from a realization that I could never beat the train to the crossing as to avoid Amy's wrath for as long as possible. When I finally did reach the bottom, I found Amy sitting on the curb, waiting for me, watching the train clack by. I sat next to her, ignoring the nasty look she shot in my direction.

"Could you play tag with a train, Amy?" I asked, forgetting her anger after a few moments. She gave me a withering look that only an older sibling can give.

"Don't be silly, you dodo."

I didn't think the question was silly, but prudently decided to keep my mouth shut. Shortly after, the train rumbled by, and the clanging bell and flashing light ceased. We hopped on our bikes and rode for home.

By the time we reached there, I'd forgotten all about the train, and raced in to turn on my favorite cartoon show, which came on after Amy's favorite. Amy usually joined me, though she professed to be too old for such childish fare, but not this time. I didn't miss her until the commercial break started trying to convince me to convince my mother to buy a certain brand of crystallized sugar masquerading as corn flakes. I thought Amy might be in the kitchen getting a snack or something and wandered in to look for her. She wasn't there, but I could see her outside, sitting on the back step. When I pushed open the screen, she didn't even turn around to look at me.

"*Flu Flu and Crazy Dog* is on, Amy."

"So what?"

"Don't you want to watch?"

"Not today, Michael."

"Watcha doin'?"

"Thinking."

"Well, I'm going back in and watch *Flu Flu and Crazy Dog*," I told her, and I let the screen door slam shut in emphasis as I retreated to the TV room. I was puzzled by her behavior, but soon got lost in the cartoons and thought no more on it.

The following day after school, I was running around with some of my classmates, playing tag of course, and waiting for Amy to find me so we could ride home. She was later than usual when she came out the door and waved to me. I ran over, pulling to a panting stop in front of her.

"Where were you?" I asked.

"Inside," she answered enigmatically. "Come on, let's go."

"We're gonna get caught by the train," I said to her, trying to make the statement as caustic as possible. To my surprise, Amy merely shrugged and walked off to the bicycle rack. Despite her nonchalance, I sensed an underlying stiffness, and, on the way out of the school yard, I asked what was wrong. Was she in trouble with her teacher?

No, she told me. There was no trouble. What was it, then? Why had she stayed after school? She was talking to a friend, she told me, then said to shut up and stop asking questions. I did so, pedaling quietly behind her until we had to dismount to walk up to the top of the hill.

As we rounded the top, Amy stopped and mounted her bike. I got a running start on mine and with a few furious pedals was past her, starting down the hill toward the railroad tracks. I reached the first curve before I realized Amy wasn't behind me. Skidding to a halt, I looked back to see her straddling her bike at the top of the hill, her gaze directed down the hill to her left.

"Come on, Amy!" I shouted and waved for her. She ignored me, or maybe she didn't hear me. I yelled again, and this time, whether she heard me or not, she stepped on the pedal, and her bike began to roll down the hill. I watched her descend, but instead of slowing as she reached me, she kept pedaling right on past, down the hill. Yelling for her to wait, I followed as fast as I dared. I passed the second place where the train tracks could be seen, saw the train already moving down them, and called out the fact to Amy. But she was disappearing around the next bend, and I didn't see her again until I got to the bottom. She was straddling her bike, watching the train go past. Her face was flushed, a strange light in her eyes. Ignoring my questions, she watched the last of the train pass, then we remounted and rode home.

Thus began a pattern that took me the better part of the week to figure out. Each day, Amy would hang around after school, doing what, I wasn't sure. Then she'd come to drag me from my tag game, and we'd ride home. At the top of the hill, she'd wait until she could see the train pass through the perspective window, then she'd ride furiously to the bottom where the road crossed the tracks. Being such a tag fanatic, I soon realized she was racing the train, but the reasons were obscure to me.

"Are you playing tag with the train?" I asked her on about the fourth day we waited at the top of the hill for the train to show itself.

"Sort of," she replied distantly, her attention on the perspective window.

"Why don't you just play with the rest of us at school?"

"Because this is different," she said, for once taking her attention off the visible portion of track and looking right at me. I was a bit taken aback by the intensity of her gaze, but I could tell she wasn't angry or anything like that, just excited in a way I'd never seen before.

"How?" I wanted to know, but didn't get an answer.

"Darn!" she exclaimed and began pumping her bike down the hill. I saw that the train was visible below, and I chased behind, realizing I couldn't catch up with her. In moments, she was out of sight around the next bend. I finally pulled up next to her at the bottom, with the train already half past.

"I'm sorry, Amy," I said, feeling guilty for having distracted her. Again she turned that new look on me, and again I saw she wasn't angry.

"It's okay," she said, and we started home.

Mother noticed we weren't coming home as quickly as we used to, and questioned us about it. Amy told her she was staying late to help a friend with a special project, and that I occupied myself playing tag until she was through. She didn't mention the train, so I thought I would.

"That's right," I cut in. "And every day we're just late enough to get caught by the train."

Amy shot me a look that Mom didn't see but that spoke volumes to me. It told me I'd better keep my mouth shut about the train. But Amy needn't have worried, for Mom didn't notice anything unusual. She was aware that the train passed daily through the valley, and if we were a little late we'd have to wait for it. She'd cautioned us enough times to keep back when we did, for the crossing had no barrier, only a warning light and bell.

But if Mom didn't suspect Amy was racing the train, she did begin to suspect something else—something I didn't understand at the time, though I was aware of the basic differences between boys and girls. Amy had been racing the train to the bottom of the hill for about a month when I chanced to overhear Mom asking her some questions one night before bedtime.

She asked about the friend Amy was staying after school to help. I held my breath, for I was fairly sure Amy wasn't actually staying after school to help anyone, though I really didn't know what she did until we left. However, Amy came right out with the name Arthur. She and Arthur, she said, were working together on a science fair project. Mom seemed to think all her questions were answered then and there, and though she did ask what the project was, I could tell she wasn't as curious about it as she was about Arthur.

I was sure Amy had lied about meeting someone named Arthur, so I decided to see for myself what she did after school each day. The next afternoon, I sacrificed my tag time and went in search of her. I wasn't very familiar with the big school where the older kids attended class, and I got lost until a teacher saw me and, perhaps suspicious that a younger kid would be wandering around where he didn't belong, asked me what I was doing. I told her I was looking for my sister, and she showed me how to get to the wing where the seventh-grade classes were. I was soon in the right hall, and presently found Amy. I was surprised when I did. There was a boy with her.

They were at the back of the classroom, where a lot of projects were set up on tables and counters. Several other students were in the room, all engaged in their projects. I sidled into the room and over to Amy. When she saw me, her face turned red. To this day, I'm not sure if it was her boyfriend she was embarrassed by or me. Maybe it was a combination of the two, but whatever it was, she hurried me out of the room and in a sharp but hushed voice told me to go back to my friends until she came and got me. I did, only slightly perturbed at her attitude. I'd gotten a good look at the boy she was with and was more concerned with him than with Amy's scolding. I don't suppose there were any distinguishing features to him, though. He was just an older kid, taller than me, slightly long legged, with a somewhat thin face and brown hair.

I did go back to where my friends were playing tag but didn't feel like joining in. I was wondering about Amy, Arthur, and the train. Before I knew about Arthur, I'd thought Amy was just staying after school as an excuse to be late enough to race the train. But if Amy had reasons for staying after school other than the train, why was she racing it? This was an imponderable question for me, and I resolved to discover the answer. When Amy finally came by to collect me, I almost blurted out an interrogation right then but stopped myself. She wouldn't have answered, or worse, she'd have given misleading answers. I'd have to discover the truth on my own.

That afternoon, however, I didn't have a chance to ask or observe anything. I don't know if Amy was angry with me for seeking her out, or if something else was bothering her, but whatever the reason, instead of waiting for the train at the top of the hill and racing to the bottom, she just rode down the hill, letting me keep up with her. The train had nearly passed, and we waited in silence for it to clear the crossing. When we reached home, she went straight to her room and stayed there until dinner. And after we'd eaten, she returned to her room and occupied herself there until it was time to go to bed.

The next morning, on the way to school, she seemed to be a little melancholy, but that evening she beckoned me from my tag game with her normal spirits. We rode to the hill and pushed our bikes up it. There we paused, both of us looking though the perspective window at the train tracks running through the valley below. While we waited for the appearance of the train, I saw Amy pull a shiny, pendulous object from her pocket.

"What's that?" I asked, leaning forward for a closer look.

"A stopwatch," she replied then told me what it was for.

"Where'd you get it?" I asked in a hushed voice. "Did you steal it?"

"I didn't steal it, you dodo!" she retorted huffily. "I borrowed it from Arthur."

"Yeah," I shot back, not to be undone. "Well, I bet he stole it."

"He did not! He got it from his father, who's the gym coach at the high school."

"What's a gym coach?"

"He teaches recess, sort of," she told me, and I knew then I had her over a barrel.

"Hah! There's no such thing as a recess teacher!" I replied nastily. Amy just looked at me like I was an idiot, though, and I was cowed. I wanted to hold the stopwatch, but Amy refused, saying I'd probably break it or lose it or something.

"Whatcha got it for?" I wanted to know.

"You'll see."

A moment later we heard the distant rumble that heralded the approach of the train. Amy watched the tracks intently, and, as the train approached, her thumb pressed down on the stem of the stopwatch. Then she was off, racing down the hill, with me dropping behind. As I neared the crossing at the bottom of the hill a couple of minutes later, I saw Amy there, examining the stopwatch. I rode over to her and made a rude noise.

"Wassamatter? You break it?

She ignored me and finished her examination.

"What time does it say?" I asked, edging over to her. She held up the watch dramatically for me to see but snatched it back before I could actually do so, stuffing it into her pocket.

"Come on, Amy," I whined.

"It says it's time to go home," she replied, hopping on her bike and pedaling away. Yelling something derogatory after her, I followed at a safe distance.

For the next two weeks, I watched as Amy timed the train's run from the spot on the tracks visible through the perspective window to the crossing at the bottom of the hill. She also calculated her own time from the top to the crossing. The train usually took eighty-three seconds to cover the distance, and Amy's best time was ninety-eight seconds. She consented to let me check my own time down the hill, but I couldn't do it in less than two minutes. Shortly after that, the stopwatch disappeared. I suppose she gave it back to Arthur. Then, for more than three weeks, she left me at the top of the hill to follow at my slower pace while she raced to the bottom in pursuit of her unuttered goal.

During this time, Mom asked me what was going on with Amy. Did I know Arthur? I answered as best as I could without revealing Amy's activities. I knew that racing with the train was dangerous and that Mom wouldn't approve, so I skirted the subject. I told her I'd seen Arthur though I hadn't actually met him. I mentioned he was the son of the recess teacher at the big school, and she gave me a curious look but didn't ask more.

Mom's questions made me a little nervous about Amy's activities. Perhaps they forced me to think more about what she was doing, about the possible dangers involved, or maybe

I was just concerned about having to hide the truth from our parents for Amy's sake. Whatever the reasons, I confronted her with my fears one day while we waited at the top of the hill for the train. To my chagrin, she all but ignored me, putting off my objections with either a shrug or glib answers that I couldn't refute. I was getting quite frustrated when the train appeared and Amy took off, racing down the hill and out of sight around the first bend.

Angry and hurt, I resolved to play no further part in Amy's foolishness. She could race the train all day and night if she wanted, but I planned to ignore her. Thereafter, for several weeks, when we got to the top of the hill, Amy would wait for the first view of the train then race to the bottom, but I merely continued to ride on to the crossing, not waiting for Amy to begin. About half the time she sped by me on the slope, and the other half I watched her skid to a stop at the crossing just moments after the train rumbled across the road. And I couldn't help but notice she kept arriving at the crossing a bit sooner each day. By the end of that period, Amy was coming around the last bend in the road just as the train crossed.

Then one day, I watched Amy slide to a stop in front of the crossing only a second after the locomotive roared through. Despite myself, my interest renewed. Excitedly, I ran over to where she sat on her bike, watching the train pass. Her face was impassive as I plucked at her sleeve and went on about how close she'd come that time. She all but ignored me as the train rumbled on. Then she turned her eyes on me but looked right through me, not seeming to hear what I said. I was hurt by her disregard, but as we left the crossing and rode home, I thought of the weeks I'd meanly neglected her efforts. By the time we got home, I apologized to Amy, and though she nodded and smiled, I could tell her attention was elsewhere.

The following day she failed to race the train. We arrived at the top of the hill about the usual time, but instead of waiting there for the train to appear, Amy just leisurely coasted down the hill to the crossing. Puzzled, I followed, calling out questions but getting no replies. When we reached the bottom the train was already well through the crossing. As we braked in front of the tracks, I asked her again why she wasn't racing. This time she looked at me and shrugged, saying she wasn't interested. I wanted to know how that could be after all the time and effort she'd expended, but she merely said she just didn't feel like it.

The next few weeks were bleak ones for me. I'd had my own interest and excitement renewed by Amy's near victory, and the fact that she'd stopped racing was a blow to me, especially since I saw myself responsible. I believed that if I hadn't ignored her efforts for the weeks I had, she'd still be racing the train. At last, after all the self-recriminations, it struck me that maybe Amy was scared.

"Chicken" was a popular epithet around grade school, but it was another thing to apply it to one's older sibling. I shied away from the realization for several days, even though I'd begun to understand there might be something to fear. I remembered the dead dog Amy and I had found in the weed-filled ditch between the road and the train tracks the year before. We'd stopped to stare at the mangled and already bloating body for several minutes, wondering what had happened. It had been hit by a car or a train, but we couldn't decide which. The body remained in the ditch until it completely decomposed—an instructive but fascinatingly unsightly and odorous lesson in biology. Thoughts of the dog preyed on my mind for a week until they burst out one afternoon.

"Amy," I panted, pushing my bike faster to catch up with her as we trudged up the hill. "Amy, are you afraid of the train? The dog...."

She shot a curious look at me that shut me up but said nothing until we reached the top of the hill. There, for the first time in weeks, she stopped and stared toward the perspective window.

"I don't think so, Michael," she said, not looking at me but at the visible lines of the tracks far down the hill. "I don't think I'm afraid. Do you?" She turned and asked the last of me, but I found it difficult to answer. I was confused by my own thoughts, not willing to trust my mouth to say the right thing. Apparently she sensed my confusion, for she turned away and again stared at the tracks.

"Come on," she said, urgency tingeing her voice. "Let's watch the train cross the road." She started down, but not so fast I couldn't keep up.

We got to the bottom in time to watch the train rush through, and as it went by, I couldn't help but feel awed by its size and power. Amy had an incomprehensible look on her face, in her eyes, as the cars thundered down the track.

Two days later, she started racing again. I was elated despite my fears, except for one thing. She wouldn't allow me to be at the bottom when she got there. I had to promise to remain at the top of the hill until the train first appeared and only start down the hill after she did. At first, I believed she was trying to punish me for my inconsideration and indifference the month before. Then it came to me that perhaps she wanted to be alone in her effort, that she didn't consider what she was doing to be a spectator sport. Only later did I realize she was protecting me in case she failed.

I was irked by the restriction, but she was adamant, so there was little I could do but comply. Even so, I knew, despite the fact that I couldn't actually see, that over the next month she gradually came closer to the tracks each time she arrived at the crossing. She took on a single-minded intensity after leaving the school each day that didn't ease until she'd raced to the bottom of the hill.

Then, one night after Mom and Dad had put us to bed, when I'd nearly fallen asleep, I heard someone softly enter my room and come over to my bed. I rolled over to see Amy standing there, silhouetted by the half-light from the door. She was dressed in pajamas, her hair slightly disheveled.

"Michael," she said quietly. "I have something for you."

"What is it?" I was puzzled, for Amy wasn't in the habit of giving me things except for birthday and Christmas presents.

She reached out her hand, and I took the object from her. I instantly knew what it was, and as I held it up to the light, I was even more puzzled and not a little frightened. It was something I'd coveted and had tried to trade for on many occasions. She'd never relented, though, and that made her presentation all the more curious.

"What's it for?" I asked, not daring to say more.

"It's for you," she said with a slight catch in her breath. "You always liked it, and I want you to have it."

"Thanks, Amy," I said lamely, feeling lost.

"I love you, Mikey," she said, bending over to hug me. Then she turned quickly and went out of the room. I lay there for some time, holding the prism up to the light from the half-opened door, watching bands of color sparkle in the glass. Still grasping the prism in my fist, I fell asleep.

The next day, Amy came to get me after school. I wasn't playing tag but was sitting on a bench, waiting for her, fingering the prism and holding it up to the sun. When Amy came up, I stuffed the prism into my pocket and followed her to the bike racks. We left the school yard and rode to the hill. We walked to the top, neither of us speaking. I sensed that today was different from yesterday. The race was going to be for real. The prism was angular in my pocket, reminding me with every step I took of every time I'd hurt my sister. I tried to speak to her, but she wasn't listening. At the top of the hill, I took out the prism, held it up to the sun, and sprayed a rainbow onto Amy's back, showering her with color. Then her back was gone, and she was pedaling furiously down the hill.

"Amy!" I cried out. "Amy!" I stuffed the prism into my pocket and took off after her. She rounded the first bend in the road and was lost to sight.

A great dread rose in me as I gave chase. Visions of the dead dog, torn and smelly in the ditch, rushed past with the scenery as I raced to the bottom of the hill, crying out Amy's name. Tears streaked my cheeks, and I was shaking so hard I could barely steer around the curves. At last, after what seemed like forever, I reached to bottom of the hill and skidded to a halt in front of the tracks.

The train was rumbling through the crossing, but of Amy there was no sign. I looked around frantically, thinking she might be off to the side, but still I couldn't see her. I had two thoughts, then, conflicting but equally terrible. One was of Amy ascending from the Earth, dressed in white wings; the other was of her crouching behind a bush or a tree somewhere on the slope above me, snickering at the stupidity of her little brother. Anger ran through my fear like hot lightning through a dark cloud. Then, as I turned to look at the train, I saw her.

She lay on the ground on the other side of the tracks, unmoving. Her bike was several feet away, one wheel spinning around and around. I moved as close to the train as I dared and peered beneath the rushing, clattering cars, fear wiping away all anger. She was on her back, but twisted slightly to one side. One of her arms was thrown across her face, and I could see blood on one of her knees.

"Amy!" I screamed beneath the train, but the clanging bell and rumbling rattle wiped out my tiny voice.

The train never seemed to take so long to pass, though it must actually have done so in a couple of minutes or less. By the time it had, I was frantic with panic. As the caboose went by, I raced across the rails to her. Yes, there was definitely blood on her. I plunged to the ground beside her, took her arm in my shaking hands, and lifted it from her face. To my intense relief, her eyes were open, and as I sat back on my haunches and began to bawl out in great huffs, she turned them on me and a small smile crossed her lips. Then she sat up and hugged me to her.

"It's all right, Mikey," she said again and again. "It's all right. It's over with. It's over."

At last she pushed me back and examined the scrape on her knee. Seeing it wasn't much, she turned back to me. I'd stopped bawling, though I was still snuffling and leaking from the eyes.

"Get your bike," she said. As I did, she picked up her own and waited for me to come back across the tracks.

Tracey Nichols

The Storm

"It's coming," Mother yelled excitedly. Her sudsy hand threw a yellow plate at the dish holder. It missed, fell and shattered on the kitchen floor with a noisy crash.

"Kids, kids, hurry! Put your shoes on, and your sweaters, too, now. Oh, Roy, it's so close, come see!" She yelped, wiping her hands on a checked towel. Stepping on crunching pieces of plate, she ran to the living room. Most country farms like this one had the living room off the back porch.

"It's a funnel cloud, sure is . . . couldn't be more than five miles off. What should we do, oh, us, open the windows?" She cleared her throat and rubbed the palms of her hands together. "Let's see, which ones, the southwest ones? I mean, doesn't the wind blow southwest to northeast, or is it the other way around?" she blurted and stammered as her sharp eyes darted from room to room. She did this during bouts of high-strung nervousness, which came often. Her tone had a more emphatic edge to it this time, though.

Father slowly eased himself out of the chair, and disinterestedly slid into his brown-leather house shoes. Striking up his pipe (which he's long since given up due to lip cancer) and padding across the floor in his boxer shorts, he was the picture of unastonished composure. My childhood gave me two visions of the contradictory truth, which is healthy for anyone, I'm sure.

The recollection must be twenty years old (when I was five and in the first grade), but some things one never forgets. That scowl on his brow as he placed the book face down (he was a knowledge-motivated man), and his muttering on that day somehow sticks firmly in my mind.

Knuckles white, gripping the sink, Mother's agitated voice rose an octave higher.

"My Lord, what are we gonna do? Quickly, kids, grab your stuff and come on. We're going to the storm cellar. . . ."

By this time, we were all bunched around the window, straining our necks to see. With a wild whoop, my eldest, buck-toothed brother exclaimed, "Look at that whirlpool a' dust. I betcha that cloud kin knock ya off yur feet!"

"It can knock the freckles right off your nose, now go! And help Kevin, too!" she hollered, patting him between the shoulder blades before he dashed off.

"Good God, Roy, it's goin' to blow us away! They say when it hits it sounds just like a train." Mother's voice trailed as she shook her head. Her eyes were wide and teary.

Trying to find our sweaters and shoes was a major chore in the bedroom I shared with my two sisters. Clothes, toys, and indescribable junk scattered everywhere. It was a wonder we didn't disappear into Junkdom for ever, where all messy kids deserve to go. My favorite red sweater was located between a night stand and the bed, crumpled into a small bundle. Shaking it out (something Mom always told me to do in case of nesting mice) I put it on and looked out the window.

The yellow-gray sky was beginning to darken to a deep grayish-black color in patches along the horizon. When I opened the window, a few drops of drizzle sprayed into my face. The stillness seemed to silence the frogs' songs in the wind on the flat plains of this southern Oklahoma farm. Even though I knew very little about tornadoes, the quiescence of the evening did not seem to fit the description of one to me. Tumbleweeds began to roll unsmoothly, like tractor tires in mud, toward the enormous, gray barn.

I was sure the possums, skunks, and owls were burrowing into more secure habitats, sensing intuitively the feeling of dramatic air pressure change. The tall, green stalks of maize were bowing their heads to the ground in reverent Hindu meditation, and the tranquillity turned into a windy, swirling backflow of activity.

A flurry of air belched forth a stench of insect spray that hung in the breeze after the crop dusters had sprayed that morning. Was it for cotton? I don't remember, but that odor and wet earth trace repelled and thrilled me, and even today still leaves me with associations of tornadoes.

Dad was fond of bringing home treats, and I grabbed the bag of lemon drops from the top of my bed on the way out. Scooping up my shoes and socks, I ran to the hall by the front door to put them on.

Mother's voice kept getting louder and louder. I suppose she was hollering at one of my siblings, Clamorous sounds came from my brothers' bedroom at the same time the animals by the four waste sheds took up mooing, quacking, gobbling, and hooting. Inside, the trills, honking, and clucking created comparable pandemonium as well. Off pitch, the sound of thunder came clashing in and managed temporarily to silence the whole lot of us.

The omen of the gods seemed to straddle the red-brick farm house that stood in the open and deserted terrain. Even though the sound frightened me, I always felt excitement before a storm. It meant we could run down to the stock pond, the one with the windmill in the center, and play in the red mud afterwards. In an oozy, sloshy slime, we pretended it was quicksand or a sizable suction cup taking us in, ensnaring us, enmeshed to our elbows. Far-gone into muddy paradise, submerged in an inanimate thick cloak, playing in the stock pond after a rain was the next best thing to mother's womb.

The windstorm became more forceful. The trees commenced doing something that looked to me like an exotic, tribal dance. I remember trying to duplicate the moves as I popped a lemon drop into my mouth.

Running outside to find Tiger, the newest, feline member of the family, I noticed the windmill was violently shaking, as if almost losing its balance. A sharp crash turned my attention to a glass, gallon milk container that we kept our fresh milk in. It had blown off the porch onto the sidewalk.

"Where are you, baby? Come on, kitty."

My blue print shirt, enveloping my skinny frame, blew up in gusts around my chin. The cows were standing together at the salt licks. The long, red hairs on their backs were fluttering in tufts and their tails were floating in smooth waves, all pointing northeast. Swirling dust blinded me temporarily. A screen door slammed, and whimpering, nervous voices came out. Mother was still inside, trying to gather her last chick beneath her wing.

"Now, Roy, don't be foolish. That tornado is on its way, and you'd be a fool not to take cover . . . please!" she chided, agitation making her jaw set just so.

"Oh, that thing isn't going to hit, Linnie. You're just being over-hysterical as usual. Why don't you just calm down? You're frightening all the kids, now."

Full lips were pursed together, his look serious. During those rough times, only the youngest children could bring a smile to my father's face. We were poor even though Dad worked overtime. Bless his heart, he had a definite calamity of spirit with too many indefinite reasons. My mother worked also (this perhaps an understatement) as a nurse at a local hospital Although it was hard labor, to sure, it was also a relief for her to get away from the free-spirited country children that we had become. Later her job turned into a midnight shift.

Many times during those months, she was angry and frustrated. I once interrupted one of her tirades by saying, "You don't care about us at all!" Viciously said, it was meant to invoke guilt within her. I was scared when I saw the family breaking up. Later that night, I heard her crying in the living room, my father's even-toned voice trying to console her, and the words were low and indistinguishable. She never got over feeling guilty for leaving the oldest kids at home alone sometimes. That was the first time I heard the word divorce.

"You just don't want to pull yourself away from that damn TV!" her voice brawled, "You self-destructive, lazy bum!"

"Maybe I will take a little break, just to get me a fresh beer. You sure could use one. You're raving mad," he said choppily, with ice in his voice. His attitude during arguments became more unaffected and bovine with each passing criticism. He sighed heavily and marched from the room with a smug look on his face.

"What a great example you set for the children. You can go to hell!" she attacked in rage.

"Aah, go on, hysterical woman. You're disturbing the reception," he stated matter-of-factly in a monotone voice.

She turned and stomped out with one last, cutting remark on her lips. "I hope the tornado splinters that easy chair, fellah!"

Lord knows, one remark was an unfair statement, for the old TV we burned hot night and day back then was strictly for the benefit of the children—a cheap baby-sitter. My father rarely had time for such luxuries. It was plain to me that there was a greater tempest indoors than out.

Overreacting is what my father called her zealous animation, but, truthfully, she was more full of life than he was, had boundless energy, and got bored easily. The county was no place for a city woman. That had been his idea, and he felt ashamed to admit his mistake.

Now she was concerned for her family—the big one she had always wanted. My dad felt trapped and unsuccessful; there was no denying it in his eyes. Life provided him with an endless supply of mouths to feed. His traditional mind told him, "If only I was rich, my wife wouldn't have to work. She'd be happy, and I could spend more time teaching Cory how to throw a ball and Jenny her ABCs."

After my mother had gained weight, she would criticize my father for bringing home too many groceries, sweets in particular.

"If you bring all that junk home, I can't help but eat it. Help me, will you? I'm addicted to sweets just like an alcoholic."

"Linnie, I'm not going to deny the kids food they like just because you can't control your appetite. Just go on a regular diet."

"Roy, you overbuy. Some of that stuff will just spoil. Do you always have to play the great provider?"

"You mean, you over-eat. You don't make use of some of that food I see you throw away. You waste instead of making leftovers from excess food."

"I'm not Suzy Homemaker that can make T-bone steak out of ground round. You expect me to be perfect, and I try as hard as I can. A brown head of lettuce is inedible!"

"But not the chocolate cake!" he threw back. So, when he refused to stop, she ate to spite him, and because she loved chocolate cake. Soon, she enveloped herself in layers of soft cushion that would protect her from her hostility, guilt, and boredom. So, they were both to blame for saying ruinous things to one another, but neither one could help the other's discontent.

What my mother had forgotten was that my father was an artist. Oh, not by profession, but he was a most excellent painter and sculptor. Eventually, he would forget this, too. New oils and canvas were spendthrift items not included in the budget. Chocolate cake and beer were, though. Food for their stomachs, but no food for their souls. So, little by little, he dried up like a twisted, empty foil tube of paint, and never said a word about it to anyone.

What my father had forgotten was that my mother enjoyed dancing. She was full of rhythm and loved to move her feet. She had learned to tap dance in the orphan's home she was brought up in. Eventually, she would forget this too. Nights out at the local "Corral J" were not in the budget, even though new jeans for the kids were. My father was not a dancer, nor did he even try to learn. Luxuries like this seemed frivolous next to the overwhelming worries of "getting by," so little by little her feet stopped tapping to the transistor radio on the kitchen window ledge.

They always forgave each other.

When she slammed the door, a deluge of pouring rain halted her steps. The children were all playing in the torrent, squealing with delight, quite forgetting all about the catastrophic tornado in the wake.

"Help me lift this, Lezley. It's heavy. We need to get in here fast."

"But what about Daddy? Isn't he coming?" Lezley asked with a look of horror coming over her face.

"Oh, I hope the wind blows that stubborn ol' goat away!" she bit, almost chewing with delight on the words.

"Mama!"

"Where Dada?" the baby boy, Kevin, asked with a slight tip of his tow-head.

"Inside, dear. He's hiding from the storm inside, but we are hiding in here. OK? He's watching TV."

"Uh, uh. Me go inside. Wanna watch TV," he whimpered, sensing the obvious uneasiness in her voice.

"Don't get bossy with me, young man, or I'll turn you across my knee. You kids never do as I say anymore. It's living out in this damn country that did it. You just run wild! Come on! Let's go. NOW!" I suppose she overused that tone and cried wolf one too many times, because it had grown somewhat ineffective.

As they opened the heavy, metal door that was almost parallel to the ground, Lezley remarked, "I'm not going in there, no siree. There's bugs and everything crawly in that place."

"Me, neither," I joined in, feeling a sweat rise to my brow. Nothing had ever seemed scarier. Every child was soon in unison. Usually, when one refused to do something, say for instance eating cabbage, invariably we all did. It was blood code and very offensive to break the pact, even if it meant severe punishment, which it usually did.

I spotted Tiger, the cat, about to pounce on a sand-colored grasshopper and swept her up in my arms.

"Ya can't crawl in the bottle any more, Tiger. It broke on the steps, look," I said, turning the cat's face to the porch.

Finally relenting, due to the intermittent rain soaking us to the bone, Cory went first. Cory and Lezley were twins, and they usually made all the important decisions for the younger ones. (I survived many bloody noses with those two.)

By now, the funnel was up against our backbones. As I turned to look at it, my insides felt like viscid and heavy. There was a crack of jagged, purple lightning filling the sky with a light show then booming deep-voiced thunder. We all screamed in accord.

The storm cellar was a sunken dugout with red dirt, now mud, packed on a concrete roof above rotten, wooden-framed walls. What light was left in the dark sky cast only enough illumination for us to see five concrete steps leading to oblivion. A black hole.

Some cried louder than others when Mother ordered us down the stairs behind her, single file. Holding on to each other, we gritted our teeth and never lost contact—well-trained elephants in a circus.

I was on the end. Something in me knew this was just as bad as any ol' tornado, and I couldn't decide which was the worst of the two evils. I let go of my sister's shirttail. When they got to the bottom, I was still at the top of the stairs, rain pelting my forehead.

"Come on, come, Jenny. Help her, Cory," Mother's alarmed voice urged frantically.

I stumbled down the steps. Cory saw the kitten poking from under my sweater, damp and wild-eyed. He suddenly bolted out the door.

"Freckles! Maaamaaah, we forgot Freckles!"

He ran full-lunged, out into the storm, wailing the dog's name over and over again. Mama ran out after him. Several minutes passed. The rest of the children cried, fearing for Father's and Mother's lives, as well as Freckles's and Cory's, repeating over and over what sounded suspiciously like the "Lord's Prayer." Not being a churchly family, that was the only prayer we knew. Those few minutes seemed like a wicked eternity.

Severe retributions overflowed on Mama's lips as she returned. She had Cory by the collar, and closed the door. Cory, with his arms full of a muddied Freckles, looked like a form of lower animal life himself. His expression told us the storm was overhead. Spankings never made him that pale.

In the meantime, we caught a whiff of Freckles, the rankest dog this side of Kansas. A short-haired, brown and white spotted terrier, he managed to chase skunks down and inevitably lose. To this day, that is a pleasant, even comforting smell to me.

Just as our fears were easing, a rat's alarmed squeak broke the stillness of the musty, grave-like quarters and made me choke on the lemon drop. With a white, utility candle and two matches Dad kept on the front shelving, our courage bolstered, and we struck one of the match sticks and lit the candle. The little flicker became a steady light and no sooner than our eyes adjusted, did we see a huge, black spider crawling on Dena's toe. (Yes, one shoe was missing—she couldn't find it amid the junk.) She shrieked and began to cry all over again.

"Stop," I whimpered. "You'll scare Tiger."

Old tin boxes, a window pane of glass, and grocery crates with their labels peeling and faded, surrounded us from all sides. We made the crates our seating in this smothering limbo.

On the right, wooden shelves appeared to be hammered into dirt walls, and held unordered rows of glass, mason jars filled with fruit preserves, green beans, and pickled somethings. The cobwebbed dungeon smelled damp and ancient. It also had a rat smell that I attributed to the grain and potatoes stored in burlap bags down there. Dad said they had a distinct smell, and he grumbled each time he threw away many half-eaten potatoes. There seemed to be an oily substance on the dirt floor, probably leaking out of a rusted piece of farm equipment that stood monster-like, snaggletoothed, and ironbound in the corner.

The rain sounded tinny on the door and seemed to beat out its urgent message for us to listen to. We all lost our voices, except for occasional streams of moaning, and in awe we waited for the sound of the train.

Dena's mouth was set in clenched and repressed fear, which was really quite hilarious in retrospect. Mother was, without a doubt, the most unnerved and emotional of us all. Probably because she had stayed up late and never seemed to sleep very long. Determined not to lose any of the flock, she counted heads. I thought that was one of the most ridiculous and silliest gestures she could have done. Maybe she was trying to keep her mind off the pulverization of the door overhead, that was by now starting to drip around the edges. Water was leaking from half a dozen places in this bottled-up purgatory. We remained for more than an hour in this condition, and I prayed silently for Dad's stubborn soul, sure he had been left for dead. We were in an interment camp, being tested for endurance by something savage and cruel. Condemned in this cave, nothing could have seemed more frightening, except for the punishing noises out of doors. Mama was our head jailer.

From the outside, I suppose we looked like a family of mice, secretly hiding ourselves in a tin can as Zeus not only pissed through a sieve but blew his potent breath upon us.

"Maybe this storm will pass, and we can all go in and have chicken and dumplings. Would you like that?" Mama whispered.

"Dena, sit on this overturned milk stool here," Mama said, trying to take her mind off spiders.

"Can't, Mama, tump over," Dena mumbled.

"Oh, I see, one of the legs is broken. Well, come over and sit on my lap, too," I noticed she always held more than one of us when she was afraid.

The tonality of the little faces brightened as the rain began to stop. My mother's beautifully gentle face was dewy and glistening in the half-light. The slight wrinkles by the side of her eyes constricted as she drew picture in the dirt with a stick to amuse the younger ones. It was obvious that she was scared to predict the storm was over. There was dirt smeared on one fleshy, apple-cheek and strands of auburn hair pasted to her thick neck. Her chest lifted and heaved softly. Then she turned to me and, with tears in her eyes, weakly smiled to comfort me. Oh, how I longed to rip out all of the fretful misery that clung to her life and take her into my arms and tell her, "Don't worry, Mama. Everything's goin' to be all right." It was on this day, so early in my lifetime, that I realized how truly sacrificial and gracious a woman she really was. I also discovered her never-ending concern and realized how purely she loved us all. Angry shouts lost their volume in my mind, and bad words she had spoken in frustration lost their meaning. In that instant, I felt free to grow toward something special, learn how to read, and run the maize fields.

The cat mewed loudly, and the dog ran from one corner of the cellar to another. Because it was such close quarters, that probably meant four or five steps. He began doing backflips. When Freckles got anxious, he would jump high in the air and twist his body in such a way that he would actually flip. Mother spanked him on the rump and scolded him.

"This smelly hold isn't big enough for you to perform now, you stinky dog!"

In order to cope with disaster, one needed a great deal of patience, coolness, and presence of mind. Mother possessed none of these qualities.

All became quiet. Wet and shivering, Mother finally opened the lid to our coffin and walked up the steps to a somewhat startling, quiet world.

One screen had been carried several yards from the picture window in front, and a few shingles from the roof were missing, too. Lawn furniture was strewn on the porch steps. The windmill had collapsed into the muddy stock pond. Tin sheds were missing their flimsy roofs. And, the treehouse, built by Cory, had not proved storm worthy, despite his boastful comments at every turn about its sturdiness.

Mother tore into the house in search of Father's body.

"No, no, Roy my darling, oooh. . . ."

As we ran into the house, the silence was unbearable. Slowly we peeked around the corner, holding our breaths. With a look of complete surprise on her face, she knelt beside the couch to touch my father's hair. There he was, with glasses atop his head, stretched out in languid stillness. His pipe was smoking on the coffee table beside the book and a can of beer. She kissed him on the lips. He was sleeping so soundly, he had missed the storm.

JIM HENDRICK

BIRD THE GOOD

IT HAD BEEN QUITE A while since I'd heard from Bird. He had written a long letter, what he called an epistle, from Italy. He was living among the magicians in Venezia. The epistle spoke of the void. How the empty spaces between people were actually teeming and alive with demons and saints. I had written back, as I always did, urging him to settle down with a good job or woman. "I have trouble standing in line," he replied, "waiting for orders. There is too much wonderful and exotic music in my head. Nothing is left for me to do but dance."

There's not the slightest doubt in my mind that my good friend, Mr. Bird, was insane. His insanity, however, was beautiful. It was appealing to me even though I did not understand it. He rarely worked or had money. If he got a job, it lasted for only a few weeks before he was fired for some outrageous activity. In Chicago, while employed in a meat packing house, he was let go for leading his fellow workers in singing as they worked. He argued that more was accomplished when everyone wasn't bored. "Bosses are not difficult to figure out," he told me later.

Money was a low priority with Bird. People, experience, freedom all rated far above money. He much preferred to trade in order to survive. In his last epistle from Venice, he mentioned trading a novel, in English, for a used but improved suit of clothes. "I am so happy each morning to put on this new look. Italian to a T. It was said of our generation that we loved to try new things." He eventually traded or gave away everything. I suppose I admired his disdain for possessions, but how long can one exist that way? I worried about him.

I must tell you that Bird had a wonderful quality that I personally miss very much. He had the rare ability to help you get below your skin. To experience the vital emotions and thoughts often trapped inside yourself. He could do this without judgment or prying. It made you feel that the world is a wider, more meaningful place. And, that your place in it—what you are, or "your music," as he calls it—is significant and real. It was a wonderful gift. I sometimes felt I was asleep til he returned and we talked. I also knew, however, that I could not endure him on a regular basis. His disorganization and intensity were too much for me.

A desire lurked in my heart that Bird would come back from Italy completely destitute. Having seen the folly in his life, Bird would give up the wayward style for a respectable office job. "I will tell him it is something new to try on," I thought. I hated so that I worried about him. I had my own life to live, after all, but he made it terribly complicated.

*

I was, of course, astonished to see him on a wide and exclusive boulevard downtown. I worked near there in a tall office building. On my way to lunch there he was, strolling out of an opulent restaurant and sliding into an unnamable foreign sports car. He, the car, the street were equal in magnificence. Bird was in embarrassingly expensive sports clothes. He sat deep in the rich leather, looking all the part of a college boy on holiday. Even from across the street, I could see his eyes were shining. He seemed to be singing a tune, probably of his own making.

He was just pulling the car away from the curb when he spotted me. I was so dumbfounded that I could not even wave. I did manage to wind through the maze of traffic.

"What do you think? Does it fit?" This was his greeting after a year.

"Huh?"

He spun around like a child making itself drunk. "The car. The clothes."

"You, or I, have gone completely crazy."

He had just driven down from New York where all the fineries had been purchased. He quickly discovered I was on my lunch break and immediately insisted going back into the fine French Cafe from which he had just emerged.

"It's too ritzy. Let's just go have a sandwich down the block."

"No sweat," he assured me. "I'm loaded."

To the haughty maitre d', he handed several bills and requested his regular table. A crisp continental accent beckoned we follow. Bird grinned lazily and waved me ahead. We passed isles of superbly decked humanity to the rear by the garden.

"I eat here every day. They have the best seafood anywhere. The Choucroute Aux Poisson is heaven. Order anything you want."

Bird stared into the lush jungle of coconut palms and all manner of elephantine greenery for a second while I adjusted myself.

He turned. "Well, what do you think happened?"

"Giant dope deal?"

"Nope. Guess again." He beamed happily at me.

"Rich relatives?"

"Very good. But not exactly. An old friend of my grandmother was filthy rich in hoarded gold and left me six million bucks."

"What?" It took my breath away. "Why?"

"She liked me when I was a kid and didn't have anyone to leave it to. Funny, the way things happen, huh?"

It took me a few weeks to find out if his story was true. Sure enough, Bird was a millionaire. His fortune, I learned, was not six million but closer to three and a half, and not in gold but public utility stocks and electronics. Bird quickly liquidated every possible asset and piled it into several banks. "I love to go into a bank and plunk down $300,000 in cash and watch all the VPs fall all over themselves to grab the account," he told me with a twinkle in his eye. It also was true that he had bank accounts all over the place. In his spacious new house one day, I counted thirty bank books. It is amazing what one can do with money.

I'll tell you true, Bird did unbelievable things with his money. By the time I saw him next, he had bought a palazzo on the Grand Canal in Venice and a one-thousand-acre estate in New Hampshire, all with servants and completely furnished. He only lived in a gargantuan old mansion in Key West. It was as far south as he could go in America. He made sure, however, that all of the servants in all of his residences were paid handsomely. He purchased a helicopter to travel to Miami to see me and shuttle us back to the Keys every once in a while. His style of life was utterly absurd.

In the time we spent together, it appalled me how much money he threw away. At first, I constantly badgered him about it. I was raised to believe that money is sacred. Money should only be used to make more money and the rest hoarded away for emergencies. I had no idea that money was a medium of exchange. Bird thought that money used to beget money bought only slavery. So he exchanged his wealth for things both tangible and intangible. He traded it to sad and ragged children for a smile. He bought fine meals at his favorite café for bums just to delight in their fateful experience. It seemed to me that this disposal of plenitude might set a disastrous trend among the patricians. As I might have surmised, no one imitated Bird the Good.

Bird was in his high-ceilinged library one day, mulling over his check books. The ancient paddle fans were turning dreamily overhead. "Do you see this?" he gleefully said to me. "I've only spent about one and a quarter million so far. It's already been eight months." He rolled his eyes and shook his head slowly. He was ebullient. Later I learned he was as deviant in accounting as in most normal functions and had actually spent nearly $1,800,000 at that point.

Shortly thereafter, he launched into the publishing business, printing books by previously unpublished authors only. He made sure no one on his staff read the books before they were off to the presses. "Everyone who wants to speak and has the courage to try should have the chance," he told his staff. Bird published poems from old people in nursing homes in the finest leather bindings. The wild, imaginative drawings of small school children were his favorite subjects. At the release of each new project he would call a news conference— he was getting a great deal of publicity for his eccentricity, primarily ridicule—to announce the first 10,000 copies would be given away free at random shopping malls around the country. Some publishing houses criticized this move severely as a shrewd marketing strategy.

Bird would appear at these giveaways, riding in like some modern Santa Claus in his helicopter, landing in the parking lot. Hopping out of the chopper, which always drew a crowd anyway, he would announce over a bull horn. He passed out the books to children, businessmen, women in tennis outfits, policemen, clerks, tax collectors, winos, hippies, Armenians, bankers, dish washers. Anyone who refused to take a book received $25, $50, $100 to take it. These carnivals gave him such delight. "Spreading the word," Bird called it.

I had a very difficult time seeing the purpose of any of Bird's behavior. It seemed to me he was merely being naive. He had the childish neglect of reality cognizant in a true saint. Most everyone thought him committable. For a short while, when his activities were capturing space in the various media, a loose knit cult developed in his name. That is where I get the title Bird the Good. These followers began turning up at his giveaways proclaiming that the essence of happiness was only found in giving away those possessions one loved most. Mothers tried to give away their children, followers passed out their clothing, some offered their bodies. It usually ended in a chaotic scene like sale days at Macy's, the followers chanting: Bird the Good is God. The police cruisers would roar in, lights flashing, sirens screaming as Bird fought his way to his chopper and escaped into the sky.

*

The hardest aspect for me to understand was Bird's disrespect for money. I love money, and I work hard for it. I, thus, treasure it. Bird did not work for a dime of his inheritance and, thus, cared nothing for it. That's how I reasoned then. Later on, thinking about Bird and the lessons I learned from him, I could at least entertain the notion of how foolish it is to spend the best part of your energy in the search for any commodity. The war goes on in me, however, that to be comfortable and experience many of the exotic lamina of life, money is essential. Sitting on the proper side of affluence, Bird still maintained: Anything that only money can buy is not worth having. I argued with him one day that he would sing a different tune without his fortune. He laughed until I was uncomfortable. "I was just as happy before, maybe more. Listen, my friend, we all want to be successful, that's all. I am eminently successful whether I am rich or poor." I can, at least, dwell on this heresy now, although I do not entirely agree.

More of my time was being spent in Miami. My job was requiring more time and energy. I was involved with a new woman. For over a month, I lost touch with Bird altogether. When I did get around to calling, he was never at home in Key West. I finally wrote a letter after three months. Still no reply. Now that he had the means, I worried about him less; besides, it was all I could do to keep my head above water in my own affairs.

The phone rang at home one evening.

"It's about Mr. Bird," began Claude, the houseman in Key West. Claude was a gentle, elderly man Bird liked very much. "Today, I received this letter. Mr. Bird says he has disposed of all his property and spent his money." The insidious worm of worry crept into my stomach. Claude continued, "Mr. Bird left the Key West house to me. He enclosed the deed with the letter."

"Where was the letter postmarked?" I asked.

"Denver."

"Is there a return address?"

"No, sir."

I began investigating Claude's news and found that all of the bank accounts were closed, the publishing house sold, the palazzo and New Hampshire estate with new owners.

It was another month before I saw Bird. It was late autumn in Miami; a time when the snowbirds begin to arrive. It is the time of year when the weather is perfect. After work one evening, I drove to the beach and walked. Ahead of me in the mist of dusk, kicking sand as he sauntered along, was my friend Bird. For several minutes I trailed behind him. The collar of his shapeless coat was turned up. He was wearing baggy khaki trousers and the heavy plain black shoes of working men. Beside us in the distant horizon, day and night were merging in a burst of purple, blue, and orange. He turned to behold it. I moved up next to him. He shifted his gaze to me and smiled.

We stood together, silently, in the vastness of the world watching day and night play like baby wildcats in the forest.

He was much thinner and visibly fatigued, except in his eyes. The eyes were scintillating as always.

"Where have you been?" I finally asked.

"Traveling a bit. My place is close by. Come on."

We walked to a large, run-down Spanish-style rooming house on the beach. One of those remnants of faded elegance lining the poorer section of Miami Beach. We traipsed up worn flagstone steps to the attic. The room was stark: a mattress on the floor, an arm chair that was ripped in the seat with wads of cotton stuffing bubbling out, an oil heater, a small wooden table with a hot plate sitting on top. I saw no refrigerator or sign of food.

Bird led me to the single chair. He treated me as regally as a visiting king. As I sat, he stood before me, the lean six feet of him, arms folded, grinning. He began, "So, what's your guess this time?"

"Crazy again."

That's what I said, but I didn't mean it. Bird's insanity was an appearance, an aspect. The world is full of partial truths. Bird was in touch with an essential, simple virtue; knowing human worth—his own and that of others.

"I gave the rest of the money away. It was always in my way. People wouldn't touch me anymore."

"But did you have to squander it like that?" I was feeling jealous that I hadn't received any of his windfall.

He grinned at me the way he did when I'd said something ridiculous. "It was a test put to me. Now I need to return to my greater task in the service of poverty." He looked more serious for a moment, then, "Don't you love this place?"

I was confused. "Wouldn't your Key West house be more comfortable?"

He seemed offended. "Look!" he said, pointing to the open bay windows taking up half of one wall. "The ocean is moving out there. Can't you hear it? I can see it in the moonlight."

I stopped to listen and heard the gentle motion. The moon, about five-eighths full, was striking the water brilliantly.

He threw himself on the bed. "I can lay here on the bed and feel like I have my very own piece of creation."

I am by no means an aesthete, but I do enjoy beauty. For me the serenity and charm of the view was more than offset by the room in which we sat.

"How could anyone want more?" he sent on. "When I was rich, I owned a lot less. Now I can concentrate on one transcendence."

He went on talking with rising intensity for some time. Adventures he had experienced in the world. People he had hurt or neglected. Opportunities gained, and lost. His language was descriptive, enchanting. I thought, "Not even death is a challenge for him. He has examined everything."

"I've been rambling. I'm sorry."

"It's so beautiful the way you talk about life. But I'm wondering what you are going to do next."

He became very quiet and dropped his head. His voice came full of pain.

"I don't know. What can I do?"

I considered practical advice for a moment but decided to say nothing. He sat, quietly absorbed on a threshold like a defendant waiting for judgment, knowing the sentence will be harsh. The room was dark save a light spray of moonlight. After a while, I got up, and when he made not move to have me stay, I left him.

Out on the street, the old people and the vagrants roamed the tiny sidewalks. The tourists never come to this section, unless they are lost, and then only to see it from the protection of their cars. I heard singing on the porch of a house nearby. A guitar playing a Spanish tune. Dirty children ran along the street. I thought of Bird the Good. The young man with the publishing business, with property and servants. It suddenly swelled in me that maybe my friend was not the supremely independent person I thought. Maybe he needed someone.

Back up the steps, I knocked gingerly on the door. There was no response. If he was asleep, I would leave. The room was quite dark, but there was a faint glow from the corner. In the corner stood a tall dressing screen that I had not seen before. The radiance came from behind it. I did not see Bird anywhere. I walked across the room.

Behind the screen was a burning candle sitting in the tangled branches of a massive piece of driftwood. The grayness of the wood shone silver in the yellow light of the candle. By this mysterious altar, on the bare floor, was Bird, bent forward like prayer. The marvelous and humble Bird the Good.

I trekked down the steps once again, this time heading for the ocean. At the edge of the tide, I removed my footgear. I moved in to let the warm water skim over my feet. The five-eighths moon was over my head. It was a cool, clear night. A good night for being alive.

The next time I made the trip up the flagstone steps, Bird was gone. Only a week had passed, but he'd moved out. There was nothing else to do but wait.

*

From here all I have are two letters from Bird and the recollections of a few people who were with him. Within a month of our last visit, I received the first epistle. Here is a portion:

It is depressingly hard to comprehend practicality when I am always reaching for tenderness and freedom, hard to be stern and profound when I believe that life is intricate and glorious. I meet so many who put on their impersonal air, and not anyone who feels they are involved in a very personal journey. Everyone seeks to be important. No one seeks to be small and accept the vast wonder of living. Plenty attend to business as usual, but no one who is almost paralyzed by magnificent beauty in infinitesimal things. So, most of the people I cross pursue prestige and wisdom, while I now find fulfillment in sweat and germs of drunks, beggars, and prostitutes.

He explained in this letter how he was traveling the country working in missions for the poor, Salvation Army stations, seedy bars, wherever the sediment of humanity settled. He spoke with great humor and affection about his friends, usually colorful and kind bums and derelicts.

His second letter followed the first by two months. He now had a traveling companion, a black man he called only Conclusion. Bird and Conclusion together were assembling a new vision.

You said to me all those times to be careful. It is such a disgusting word. Is there anything more dreadful than being careful and missing the spontaneous love and excitement that exists? We learn to keep to ourselves, never allow the real passions to escape. Life can be a coffin, a living lifelessness.

With my new friend Conclusion, I have explored the barest essentials of bodily existence. We grovel, beg, work, mop up the vomit of men we meet. We also sing, lie in the sun, care for sad-eyed souls. I am altogether full. I could not be more happy.

This was the last letter I received. It was written on a brown paper bag. It is the most involved statement Bird ever made. It has subjects, subheadings, arrows, drawings, as well as grease stains, telephone numbers, and random rips in the paper. The ending is concise.

> How we all fear suffering. The very thought of sacrifice and pain drives men to any means of relief. If we could only understand that only through suffering can we ever be blessed with true wisdom. The wisdom of a broken heart and empty stomach. The gain in your soul is worth the temporary discomfort.

I learned that Bird had many friends. I found this out mostly through Conclusion, who was sent by Bird to tell me. No one as generous with himself as Bird could help but draw people. Some came for selfish, neurotic reasons, but Bird accepted everyone without question. Charity was a quality he never had to learn.

I remember walking with him once and running into a wealthy creep we had gone to college with. He was irritating, constantly bragging even though his life consisted primarily of spending his father's money. In my book he was zero. I told Bird after the fellow left what I thought of him.

"What kind of attitude is that?" It never occurred to me that he could consider the idiot a true friend. "I suppose everyone that doesn't suit must go? It's easy to love the lovable but damn hard to love mean, boastful, shallow people."

"It's normal to love a villain, at least for awhile," I told him, "but it's unimaginable to me to let jerks like that have your friendship. It's a waste of time. He's a gnat."

He looked at me quite seriously. "You think too much of yourself. You think its okay to be buddies with an enemy. Anyone who feels strong could say that. It's always been a tribute to make a friend of a strong enemy. It takes more than vanity to love the weak, or the . . . gnats."

Conversations with Bird inevitably broke below the surface. I was not used to it. Sometimes I would be angry, other times frustrated, often ignoring. For all the life and insight Bird bestowed on me, I must say I missed so much. Like most of us, I survived by retreating within myself.

I shared this feeling with Conclusion as we sat in my apartment. It was almost spring. It was then, sitting in my comfortable, secure surroundings, that Conclusion told me Bird was dead. He had caught pneumonia in a coal mining town in Kentucky. They had been helping the Salvation Army with relief for striking miners. He worked for several days, coughing violently with a tremendous temperature. He waved off attempts to care for him, saying there were many others who needed the medical attention. Finally, he collapsed and died a week later in a tiny hospital in the mountains.

After telling me the story, Conclusion handed me an envelope Bird said must be personally delivered.

> Sorrow is with us always, but so is laughter. It is easier to remember the sad hours than it is to give life to the happy ones. Such a shame that tears should flow naturally, but laughter, genuine rejoicing, require such effort. It is important then to cooperate with the buoyant side of ourselves. Not to stress too much a person's work, like a biographer. But to focus that

energy gathered from another to spark glee in someone else. Remember, my friend, that our struggles will fade away, but the happiness we leave lives on forever.

As I read this last word from Bird, the light of a spring day was inching into the room. There was sadness and loss, but also there was a smile on my lips. I could not think of Bird and not smile. My mind was saying why? Why is he gone? It was incomprehensible. Then a thought crept in whispering so low I had to be still and listen: "Why are any of us here at all? Is it not so much why, as how." That, I believe, is what Bird would have said.

Richard M. Bolling

Easter Tuesday

I DON'T TELL STORIES FOR a living, but you have to *do something* while you're flat out of a job. I can think of one story right off the bat, immediately, that is, that happened at Shipley's. It's a small restaurant on West Gray and Dunlavy down in Houston's Montrose area.

Everyday at Shipley's, the poet would arrive, *punc*-tu-al at nine, clump up to the counter, and sit on one of the pedestals they call stools, and then talk to anyone who sat up there. Anyone was usually Lizzie. But this isn't a story about the poet. It's a story about a robbery at Shipley's, and at the end, the poet shoots the young kid who robs the register. That's later on, of course, but I wanted to tell you this now so you would *not* be surprised. I have a phobia about surprises now. Since I was let go. *They* said, Gable, we don't need you anymore That is, we don't need your services anymore You're a *fine* technician though Fine Good worker We'll refer you Don't bother cleaning out your desk Yes sir Fine worker. I heard that three times. From Mims then Stokes then Rowland, the big boss. Three fine workers. Yes sir.

Now Shipley's. At Shipley's Tuesday. I've told you that it's a little restaurant and that it has a bar, formica-topped, and pedestal stools. It also has a jukebox, cigarette machine, tables (formica-topped) not in rows, booths by the front window, waitresses, minorities sweating in the kitchen, sweating on their backs. You can see them through the opening where they put those steaming greasy orders. The poet comes in at nine. Now, the morning of the robbery, the waitress with the penciled eyebrows took his order. I don't know her name, I don't know *any* of their names, actually, but pencil eyebrows has a crooked, sneering way of turning her lips, always painted red, and she looks hard as a boiled egg in her white uniform. She's a tough eggshell with powder on her face and leering eyes. The poet, though, has his boulder-size boots tucked under the counter and, knowing the menu by heart, he never takes his eyes away from her as he orders. He even *thinks* while looking into her face. He told me he receives terrific enjoyment from that. That morning, his leather pouch was slung under his flat shoulders and I remember how heavy it looked as he clunked it down there. I had always thought it was his purse. Not his holster.

I'm sitting there alone. Not very usual because someone usually sits with me. The stricken, the drunken, the early risers, the bohemians, the punks, the degenerates, the underhanded, the lazy; in short, the clientele, like to hear me talk. And it was exactly that way in Alabama. They all like to hear me. I can understand that well enough. Back in 'Bama, as we say, men still sit and *con*verse in front of rural stores and their country houses, just like on television. Believe me. And there's not a grain of truth to their stories. We call it fiction. And that's exactly what this is. Fiction. *I've* never heard of Shipley's being robbed. At any rate, on that day, I had been sit ting there anywhere from one to two hours, reading all that good news in the *Chronicle,* the *Post, USA Today,* the *Herald,* and a stack of papers two feet high. Sitting with my arm on them like on a windowsill and sipping coffee out of one of those mugs you inspect to see if its clean. I sat and read the top paper around my elbow.

We were the only customers that day at nine. Everyone else left before eight o'clock because it was Tuesday, Easter Tuesday I call it now. Two of us on Easter Tuesday. I'm living on unemployment, and the poet's working at night as a watchman. After a while, this black man (I singled myself out in 'Bama using that term) named Lizzie shuffles in wearing his elastic suspenders, polyester plaid pants, and his Lone Star hat, greasy as hell. Lizzie's a very likable short man, but he whines like a kid when he talks—a Southern whine, an Aunt Jemima whine—and he calls pencil eyebrows by some nickname—it's different every day—then slides onto the stool and sets down a large grocery bag. The poet wipes the coffee from his mustache and shakes Lizzie's hand than wipes his pants. Pencil eyebrows gets irritated with Lizzie because of his voice, whining like out of a play school. She plops the pale green note pad in front of him and stares full at him until he orders, moving her crooked lips. But Lizzie wants to sell the watermelon he has in the bag. She's getting hot. Do you want some breakfast or not? she says. I don't know Miss Ma'am he says Don't you want some of this good watermelon? he says. No she says. Now do you want to order? He adds Can't get 'em whole for two dollars like this. They're fine fine watermelon. Are you going to order or not? she says. Yes'm. But you know I shouldn't really be selling watermelon Because I'm black you see. You know black people and watermelon. What do you want? she says. Coffee? He says That's fine Miss Ma'am. *Now* do you want to order? she says. That's fine Miss Ma'am he says. Well? she says. I just wanted to tell you he says That I promise I won't bring up the watermelon again Even though it is the sweetest one I've *ever* seen. What do you want? she says. She writes it down on her green note pad—two donuts and coffee—shaking her head. When she leaves, Lizzie continues about the watermelon, then she knits her eyebrows together and points at him and says Don't talk to me about those again. Do you hear *me?* And Lizzie didn't talk to her about those again.

Two punkers had come in close behind Lizzie, and while Lizzie talked, they sat behind the cigarette machine beside the door. I can't see them on the other side of the machine, and I don't want to lean away from my two foot stack of papers. Actually, they *rolled* in, with black skates on their feet. The thin one is a young male with a shaved head except for one-inch of hair just above the back of his neck. One-inch and blonde. The female is older, much older, thirty or thirty-five, unnatural black hair, zig-zag cut, a black sleeveless shirt, and white *angular* pants. Strange and beautiful though. I lean away from my papers, mug in hand, attempting to see her, and she's facing me as I lean out of balance from the booth. I lean back. She was looking at me and half-smiling, as if I had done something silly, in a masculine way. Like a silly male comment or gesture, interpreted as *so cute*. I get the same look when I introduce myself to women, I say I'm Clark Gable and they say *No, Not* Clark Gable and I say It is Clark Gable and they say Are you telling me the truth? and I say Yes and they say You don't *look* like Clark Gable. Very bright statement.

I cannot understand why I must *look* like Clark Gable. Now that *would* be a long shot. I caught hell at the office for it. Everyone said Well You don't *look* like him. Maybe if I had been born earlier they would want him to look like me. I hear Gable collected unemployment too. He deposited it in a savings and his chauffeur drove him home. I wonder, I just wonder what they would say at Shipley's if I sat here in my work pants and T-shirt, like everyday, and ate and then called my limo to take me home to River Oaks. And then what if I left a bad tip? Well, that would be just like the rich. They give us apartments to build or skyscrapers to construct or they order us to find oil, telling us we need all of that to keep the world running and in good order. While they sue the fuck out of each other for millions or they *settle* for twenty million and make their business pacts on patios. And after that they die or *kill* themselves. Then here we are. Stuck with their world that we helped them create. That's like a bad tip. The poet told me he wrote about that.

> The rich dream dreams like the Poet
> But His eyes are towards the sun.

Which is why I remember this day as Easter Tuesday because my eyes keep coming back to it.

Now the big waitress rose and approached the punkers' booth. I do not use the word *big* trivially for this woman. Over six-and-a-half feet tall with black hair and a face that would turn you to stone, a compressed face, a *smushed* face at best. She wore Nikes on her feet so she never looked like she walked heavily, instead she seemed cushioned on every step. When I think of her, I think of her as stepping *over* the tables, the longest strides, the elastic in her pants exposed and rolling with her walk, and her blouse hanging over her belly. There was nothing kind *about* her. But nothing mean either. An expressionless face of enormous power that took your order and *knew* you were aghast at her size. And the punkers were no different. They were quiet when she laid the menus on the table asking Coffee? to which they nodded their heads. Then ordered. At that same moment. And as I sat there holding my mug up for my waitress, a squat kind woman with lavender-tinted hair protected by a hairnet, with my arm on my two-foot stack of papers I watched the big waitress move and roll at the hips and shrug when she wished to shrug and talk when she wished to talk, her voice like a hillbilly's. Taking orders and making no bones about it.

I remember that the punkers, of course, noticed the lack of music in the place. The female punker stood and rolled over to the jukebox in front of me. Then pencil eyebrows says that they can't wear skates in the restaurant. At that the punker does not look at pencil eyebrows, as if she did not hear, then proceeds calmly to untie her skates, dropping them beside the jukebox. She doesn't look at me. She doesn't look at anyone. I'm reading the *Herald* on the top of the stack and I hear the coins drop into the machine, then I see her pressing buttons, her mouth open, her head bobbing a little like she is listening to music. Then she picks up her skates and walks lightly to the booth, walking in front of the two boys that come into Shipley's. I suppose it depends on what you call boys, but these have no trace of hair on their white faces. One boy has dark hair, fleshed out and tall for his age, and I see from the back of his belt that his name is Henry. They sit at the center table. Both wearing jeans. Henry has his back to me. The other one is thin with a black T-shirt, no writing on it, straight and thin pale blonde hair to the neck all around. He is thin everywhere, every feature, his arms, his legs, even his chest.

I must have been absorbed in my two foot stack of papers or looking at the punk couple too much or thinking about how I didn't give a damn about anyone because when you're unemployed you think like that. I must have been in some state where I didn't really *see* those two. For what they really were. Robbery candidates. Henry and the thin boy. I remember looking at Lizzie eat his donuts, looking back at my paper. Mindless I suppose. The poet told me later that he didn't miss that they were up to something, that combined fearful and strutting walk, acting *too* ordinary. At the time he was scratching his mustache and staring over at them and I would see the poet's face, and Henry's belt, then my paper. Doesn't really matter if I realized what they were or not. I would have stayed there anyway. If they would have come in with swords dangling by their sides and daggers in their hands I would have stayed. The days were passing *that* slowly. They acted much older than their age, except once, when the big waitress handed them their menus. They surveyed her from top to bottom, bottom to top, like they were looking at a mountain, "We have to climb *that?*" and their jaws nearly fell out of their sockets. Spoke like kids when they ordered. Ordered the same meal, Breakfast Special.

Well, after the waitress returns to the bar, Lizzie turns to them, the tips of his boots touching the floor at the pedestal and he makes an inquiry. He whines Do you boys want some of the sweetest watermelon that you *ever* tasted? Henry shakes his head. The thin one faces Lizzie saying No man no. Lizzie says Now you look like two strong boys like I used to be at your age about five years ago. Lizzie winks at the poet then continues And it's gonna get real hot today. Man it's hot already. So maybe it might be good while you're out playing or *gettin some,* if you know what I mean to have some watermelon just sitting so sweet in your mouth. Well a commercial direct from New York couldn't have done better than that. The thin one's packing a pistol around his ankle, but he's the one who can't resist. He asks to see it. So Lizzie unbags it carefully, cradling it in his long black hands like his first born, and he displays a medium-sized watermelon twice as big as his head. The thin one feels it with his fingers, Lizzie's holding it out to him, and the thin one says Is it hard? Lizzie turns to the poet and says Now tell me Have I ever sold one that *was*n't hard? That wasn't the best one you ever tasted? Hard as a rock on the outside and juicy sweet inside? The poet smiles at Lizzie to keep him going then Lizzie turns to them and says Feel it man Feel it Hard as hell Hard as anything you'll get with a woman. They laugh at that. I can see Henry's shoulders shaking with laughter. But they don't want any. Lizzie tries some more lines. Still don't want any. He grunts and thumps it back in the bag.

After that they just stayed quiet. The female punker had loaded up the jukebox until *next June* with quarters, and the boys ate quickly, obviously listening to the jukebox, leaning towards each other over the table. The female punker walked lightly up to the jukebox again, though it was far from finished, and she leaned over it, sticking her butt behind Henry. They watched her for some moments. I was looking at them. They watched her lean and strain all the angles on her white pants, then they watched her walk lightly back to her booth. But at that moment, right when her pants were straining the greatest and their eyes were round as saucers, I got mad. Flaming mad. Mad at everything. Mad as a dog. Absolutely furious that she exploited herself. That's how I viewed it. Exploitation. Leaning a little more than she had to. Now I believe in God, but I'm not a saint. Not now. Used to be, but not now. Not since I started to work for a living. What I'm saying is, I usually don't get mad at men following women's asses like they have a penis in their heads instead of a brain. I usually don't mind that. But I was furious that she exploited herself. And I was almost consumed when I thought of them looking at this older body with those new pubic bodies of theirs. And from there it was a journey into exploitation itself. I was thinking about the rich again. Breaking it down. Then thinking about myself. This was nothing new, you understand, I knew that I was exploiting myself the day I started to work in this town. But madder than hell. That's what I was. I could have cussed out anyone. Could have cussed out my old boss for *hiring* me. I should have *been* a saint. Should have been "Living off faith for seven years" as this one nun said who didn't make a dime. But like I said, this was nothing new. hardly. But I had reached the apogee of my anger, the apex, the hilt. I held myself totally responsible. And everyone else too. Everyone I ever saw. From the punker with the one-inch hair down his neck, to pencil eyebrows, to the minorities smashing spatulas on the grill, to the writers who wrote the news that day in that two foot stack under my arm. Just furious. And when that kid finally robbed Shipley's, I was on fire. Let me tell you how it happened.

You know how time can pass from slow to fast because your mind wanders. That's what happened. The thin one walked to the register to pay the check. I was working on my fifth cup of coffee, still mad, still irritated at everybody and nobody, at everything and nothing, still mad like that, and I was leaning on my two-foot stack of papers completely absorbed, though, with the design of a particular napkin lying on my table. Some song played on the jukebox. Well I may not have known that he had the gun out and was robbing the register until I heard him quietly talk to the waitress. She must have thought he was joking. I *think* he was even trying to rob the register, with pencil eyebrow's help, with no one knowing. But when he talked to her everyone knew, and I *think*, I *believe* everyone knew at the same time. And that's what caused him to fire. My waitress, the kind one with the hairnet, had backed up right into the hot coffee maker, and when she jumped away from it he fired. He was really scared. You could tell that. Because when the gun went off, it went off twice, that's how *twitchy* his fingers were, he missed her by a good ten feet. But he hit the big waitress. At first I thought she just fell from dodging the bullets, but we found out later that she was hit. Badly.

Well, she fell behind the counter and, let me tell you, unless you've actually *heard* a *gun* go off inside, you won't really understand. But right when he fired everyone ducked. No one was down on the floor. But I bent over the table and Lizzie was under the counter and I could hear the punk girl scream once. *Every*one ducked. Even the kitchen help ducked. Except for the poet. I suppose that makes sense because he's the hero of the story, in a way. The poet remained sitting, crouched slightly though, but his head was high, and I remember his coffee cup still being in his hands, setting it down slowly afterwards. And after these shots, he never took his eye away from the kid. He watched his face the entire time, even when the kid told him to turn around Turn around! all he did was shake his head slowly and stare at him, studying him, not with those repelling eyes that manipulative people use but with those quiet observing eyes that only the poet has. Now the thin one waved the gun at pencil eyebrows behind the register. Her lips curled at him. That's when I realized I didn't see Henry. I never thought to look

189

outside, where he was, in the car and warming it up. Instead, I just knew that Henry disappeared. But the thin one *was* scared. And I think the poet made it worse for him. Because while pencil eyebrows scowled and emptied the register and while the big waitress lay on the floor, silent as a bear and no one helping her, while all that happened, the poet just watched. And the robber even screamed again at him, threatened him with the gun. But he realized that the gun was as effective as a spoon right then.

And I suppose he might have just taken the money and left for his death at the door, with nothing in between, if it had not been for two incidents. One which nearly cost me my life. The first incident was someone let a fart go. No one knows, still, which one of the punkers fired it. The poet contends it was the girl because he actually heard her barely say Excuse me. But Lizzie *knows* it was the boy with the one-inch hair because the fart was so loud. It *was* loud too. But that can happen under stress, when the body doesn't have control Well no one laughed about it but the kid. He chuckled, like someone let one out in the classroom, or had farted in a church. But right afterward, he was scared again and he didn't grin again until he turned around and stuffed some of the money in his pocket. Then he grinned like it was very funny, like it was very funny that he had us all by the balls, which he did. That's when the second incident occurred. I heaved my mug straight into the floor and smashed it as hard as I could, mad as hell again. Mad at his grin. Even the poet turned around at that. I stood up. I had a forcefield around me. For about two seconds I was invincible. Surprised he didn't fire at me, but I was up and screaming at him. I told him that he was a son of a bitch, a *young* juvenile son of a bitch for shooting a gun around like that. I told him What the fuck are we supposed to do? Watch you rob the shit out of this place? And I kept saying You mother fuckers You mother fuckers You come

190

in here and do whatever the fuck you want to Well one day somebody will *slit your throat* for doing whatever the fuck you want to. I told him he was a criminal and a degenerate and a goddamn pussy watcher and a fucking atheist. Well he became even more scared than I was, standing there. He started looking around like there would be some sort of uprising. Henry sounded the horn outside. And he started backing out of the place. Like each one of us had guns. All I could see was his back as he backed up to the door. Everyone watched him, and after that speech it looked like everyone was ready to pounce on him, to lunge after him, like he was in an Asian jungle. He was paranoid. I would have been too because it *did* seem like everything was leaning on him. The car horn sounded outside again. Twice this time. He had some money that he held against his chest and, when he figured he was far enough to run for the car he turned around and literally ran into the door, smashing his face against it because it wouldn't swing easily. He had judged the distance wrong. Well, while he pushed the door open with his shoulder and his face, the poet stood up in one motion sliding the pistol from his sack like a holster and, raising then lowering it in an arc, he shot. With a roar louder than any gun I've ever heard, inside or out.

The story is that there were two dead and none wounded. Oh I know everyone will remember that day, Easter Tuesday, if they were there. If you can call *that* a wound. I didn't see the poet for three weeks after that. Pencil eyebrows said they took him to jail, but in the *Post,* it said that no charges were pressed. I don't suppose it was self-defense, but I don't suppose it was malicious either. The strangest thing was that when I saw him after that three weeks, he came down and sat with me, and we talked until about mid-afternoon. That's breakfast and dinner. He said that he wouldn't have shot the kid if I hadn't stood up and incited him, so to speak. He even said that he quit his job after the robbery. About a week after. Told me about his last night on the job, but that's another story. Anyway, he said he was ready to starve after I made that speech. I suppose I can understand that. When you're unemployed you only give a damn about the essentials, and after a while, you stay sick all the time because you don't eat right. I don't know though. Sometimes I wish I would never open my mouth again.

Essay

PHILLIP LOPATE

IN THE HERE AND NOW

THE ARGUMENT OF BOTH THE hedonist and the guru is that if we were but to open ourselves to the richness of the moment, to concentrate on the feast before us, we would be filled with bliss. I have lived in the present from time to time, and I can tell you that it is much over-rated. Occasionally, as a holiday from stroking one's memories or brooding about future worries, I grant you, it can be a nice change of pace. But to "be here now" hour after hour would never work. I don't even approve of stories written in the present tense. As for poets who never use a past participle, they deserve the eternity they are striving for.

Besides, the present has a way of intruding whether you like it or not; why should I go out of my way to meet it? Let it splash on me from time to time, like a car going through a puddle, and I, on the sidewalk of my solitude, will salute it grimly like any other modern inconvenience.

If I attend a concert, obviously not to listen to the music but to find a brief breathing space in which to meditate on the past and future, I realize that there may be moments when the music invades my ears and I am forced to pay attention to it, note after note. I believe I take such intrusions gracefully. The present is not always an unwelcome guest, so long as it doesn't stay too long and cut into our time for remembering.

Even for survival, it's not necessary to focus one's full attention on the present. The instincts of a pedestrian crossing the street in a reverie will usually suffice. Alertness is all right as long as it is not treated as a promissory note on happiness. Anyone who recommends attention to the moment as a prescription for grateful wonder is only telling half the truth. To be happy one must pay attention, but to be unhappy one must also have paid attention.

Attention, at best, is a form of prayer. Conversely, as Simone Weil said, prayer is a way of focusing attention. All religions recognize this when they ask their worshipers to repeat the name of their God, a devotional practice which draws the practitioner into a trance-like awareness of the present, and the objects around oneself. With a part of the soul, one praises God, and with the other part, one expresses a hunger, a dissatisfaction, a desire for more spiritual contact. Praise must never stray too far from longing, that longing which takes us implicitly beyond the present.

I was about to say that the very act of attention implies longing, but this is not necessarily true. Attention is not always infused with desire; it can settle on us most placidly once desire has been momentarily satisfied, like after the sex act. There are also periods following over-work when the exhausted slave-body is freed and the eyes dilate to register with awe the lights of the city; one is too tired to desire anything else.

Such moments are rare. They form the basis for a poetic appreciation of the beauty of the world. However, there seems no reliable way to invoke or prolong them. The rest of the time, when we are not being edgy or impatient, we are often simply disappointed, which amounts to a confession that the present is not good enough. People often try to hide their disappointment—just as Berryman's mother told him not to let people see that he was bored, because it suggested that he had no "inner resources." But there is something to be said for disappointment. This least respected form of suffering, downgraded as a kind of petulance, at least accurately measures the distance between hope and reality. And it has its own peculiar satisfactions: why else do we return years later to places where we had been happy, if not to savor the bitter-sweet pleasure of disappointment.

Moreover, disappointment is the other side of a strong, predictive feeling for beauty or appropriate civility or decency. Only those with a sense of order and harmony can be disappointed.

We are told that to be disappointed is immature, in that it presupposes having unrealistic expectations, whereas the wise man meets each moment head-on without preconceptions, with freshness and detachment, grateful for anything it offers. However, this pernicious teaching ignores everything we know of the world. If we continue to expect what turns out to be not forthcoming, it is not because we are unworldly in our expectations, but because our very worldliness has taught us to demand of an unjust world that it behave a little more fairly. The least we can do, for instance, is to register the expectation that people in a stronger position to be kind and not cruel to those in a weaker, knowing all the while that we will probably be disappointed.

The truth is, wisdom is embittering. The task of the wise person cannot be to pretend with false naiveté that every moment is new and unprecedented but to bear the burden of bitterness that experience forces on us with as much uncomplaining dignity as strength will allow. Beyond that, all we can ask of ourselves is that the bitterness not cancel out our capacity to still be surprised.

More from Phosphene Publishing Company

Phosphene Publishing Company publishes books and DVDs relating to literature, history, the paranormal, film, spirituality, and the martial arts. For other great titles, visit

phosphenepublishing.com

A young state tax attorney decides to follow his dream of becoming an international photojournalist, moving with his new bride to El Salvador to cover its civil war. With the help of a few contacts, he becomes part of the freelance photographer ecosystem, going out daily to cover newsworthy events in the "low intensity conflict." Navigating an often stultifying bureaucracy, as well as the country's rugged physical terrain, he gradually adjusts to his new, often dangerous work environment. Both his professional and the war's courses evolve over a couple of years, culminating in an intersection that directly challenges his commitment to his dream.

It's World War I, and the fate of Africa lies in the hands of eccentric Royal Navy commander Geoffrey Spicer-Simson, who is ordered to destroy two ships on Lake Tanganyika that give the Germans military control over the continent. But that may be easier said than done. To get there, Spicer-Simson and his men will have to drag two 40' gunboats over desert torn with ravines, through tsetse-infested swamps, and across a 6,000-foot range of mountains. Undaunted, Spicer-Simson forges ahead, but can his men accept the leadership of a pretentious braggart who names his gunboats *Mimi* and *Toutou*, is completely covered with tattoos, and wears a leather skirt instead of a uniform? And if the journey to the lake isn't bizarre enough, imagine what happens when they get there and meet the Germans in mortal combat on the high seas in the middle of Africa! A non-fiction novel, *Lord of the Loincloth* is the humorously adventurous account of one of the 20th century's strangest heroes and his extraordinary quest for redemption.

Award-Winning Drama

It is the dawn of the 20th century, and infamous magus of black magic Aleister Crowley and poet William Butler Yeats contend for control of the Hermetic Order of the Golden Dawn. Their confrontation, based on real-life events, draws in Bram Stoker, author of Dracula, famous Irish revolutionary Maud Gonne, celebrated Victorian actress Florence Farr Emery, and mysteriously veiled author Fiona MacLeod, who is much more than she seems. Magic, seduction, and ambition collide as each strives to achieve his or her desires and dreams, until Fiona, in a prescient trance, confronts each of the others with their inner motivations and passions, sealing their fates.

As the last day of WWII unfolds inside the Sulphur Spring Inn, confused mayhem whirls around proprietor Sarah Robinson. Sarah drives her family crazy, but her ditzyness disguises a kindness big enough to cement her family together despite the heavy-handed approach of her temperamental husband, Evan, who is running for congress. To make matters worse, Evan can't stand the idea of his older daughter being courted by a soldier, but she is, and the young couple plans to wed that very day. Mixed up in the confusion is a younger daughter infatuated with a cosmopolitan older sergeant, a mischievous boy, and a wisecracking custodian. And when Sarah throws in a few bottles of Dr. Snaketoe's Lightnin' Elixir, watch out!

From a comic yet telling refiguring of August Strindberg's Miss Julie to a man discovering the daughter he never knew, these eleven Plays that Pop! explore the importance of human connections as we struggle to make the most of life. Along the way, you'll meet poet William Butler Yeats being confronted by his lost past, a woman on edge hiding a terrible secret, an army patrol facing the ultimate confusion of war, a man in airport limbo, and characters poking fun at the very notion of plays. And don't forget the missing Putty Sing! Whether you're interested in a good read or are looking for wonderful characters to people your stage, there's something here for every taste and every theater budget.

www.ingramcontent.com/pod-product-compliance
Lightning Source LLC
Chambersburg PA
CBHW060644260626
47161CB00008B/2987